Praise for The

"*The Deep Heart* is an invitation to discover our sacred calling and unveil the core of our very being. Tapping into our natural curiosity and wisdom, John Prendergast guides us on a transformational journey from head to heart—and to the full and pure essence of love."

TARA BRACH, PHD
author of *Radical Acceptance*

"With tender clarity, John Prendergast draws us deeper on every page. A master teacher and beautiful writer, he lays out a clear path to our true home, and then walks it with us with practical heartfelt suggestions. This book is profound, powerful, and true. What a gem."

RICK HANSON, PHD
author of *Buddha's Brain: The Practical Neuroscience of Happiness, Love, and Wisdom* and *Hardwiring Happiness: The New Brain Science of Contentment, Calm, and Confidence*

"*The Deep Heart* is a beautifully written and masterful guidebook that eloquently shows us how to recognize and embody our essential wholeness in everyday life. Both profound and practical, this seminal work reveals the road we all must travel to embody our potential as fully alive and authentic human beings. A must-read!"

RICHARD MILLER, PHD
author of *The iRest Program for Healing PTSD: A Proven-Effective Approach to Using Yoga Nidra Meditation and Deep Relaxation Techniques to Overcome Trauma; iRest Meditation: Restorative Practices for Health, Resiliency, and Well-Being*; and *Yoga Nidra: A Meditative Practice for Deep Relaxation and Healing*

"*The Deep Heart* is a beautiful, wise, and practical guide to opening to our true nature, guiding us toward waking up, as well as down and in. Integrating and distilling wisdom teachings and his own insights and inner explorations, John Prendergast has translated complex information into a clear, accessible, and contemporary form. The meditations and inquiries are wonderful invitations to explore the depths of the heart for ourselves. I highly recommend *The Deep Heart* for anyone who wishes to embody their true nature as loving awareness."

LAUREL PARNELL, PHD
author of *Rewiring the Addicted Brain with EMDR-Based Treatment*
and *Attachment-Focused EMDR: Healing Relational Trauma*

"If, as you read this exquisite book, you feel into the depths from which the author writes, you will find yourself drawn into your own depths from which healing and wisdom arise."

ROGER WALSH, MD, PHD
professor of psychiatry, philosophy, and anthropology, University
of California at Irvine, author of *Essential Spirituality: The
Seven Central Practices to Awaken Heart and Mind*

"*The Deep Heart* leads us on a journey of awakening from head to heart, where it becomes safe for the heart to freely shine. This book is a deep dive into the heart of who we really are. John Prendergast offers us beautiful words and unique forms of meditative inquiry, so that we can directly experience the Deep Heart, which is so needed in our world today."

LOCH KELLY, MDIV, LCSW
author of *The Way of Effortless Mindfulness*

"This is a wise, inspiring, beautifully written book. It points to our true nature, and to the love, compassion, and acceptance that naturally arise in us when we experience who we really are. The deep love that motivated the writing is present on every page and has the gentle power to deepen and open the heart of the reader."

JUDITH BLACKSTONE, PHD
author of *Belonging Here, Trauma and the
Unbound Body,* and *The Enlightenment Process*

"A book of great wisdom and heart from an authentic and experienced teacher of Presence. John's wise, loving, and deeply insightful words about meeting our raw experience with honesty, courage, and grace will be of immense benefit to people all over the world."

JEFF FOSTER
author of *The Way of Rest* and
The Joy of True Meditation

"*The Deep Heart* carries the taste and flavor of an author who has himself spent a lifetime immersed in the Deep Heart where soul and spirit meet. This book is a truly elegant and practical road map that seamlessly weaves soul work into the timeless wisdom of spiritual practice."

ROGER HOUSDEN
author of the Ten Poems series, and *Dropping the Struggle: Seven Ways to Love the Life You Have*

"The spiritual journey does not end with awakening to the Infinite, but begins a life lived more and more consciously from the loving and immanent Presence that has awakened itself within. Writing with exquisite clarity and compassion, John Prendergast explores these two dimensions of the awakening process in his newest book, *The Deep Heart*. His intimate knowledge of the human psyche through his many years functioning as a gifted psychotherapist and educator deeply informs his work and writing as a spiritual teacher.

John writes from authentic experience of both the challenges of being a conditioned human being and the freedom of simply *Being*. Through numerous guided meditations and exercises, he invites the reader to deeply inquire into the truth of experience, and to allow the wounded heart to be touched and transformed by the Deep Heart that is undivided and whole. John approaches with great sensitivity the human experience through the single Eye that sees the inseparability of the Heart of Awareness and its expressions as life itself."

DOROTHY HUNT
spiritual director of Moon Mountain Sangha
and author of *Ending the Search: From Spiritual Ambition to the Heart of Awareness*

"Psychotherapist and spiritual teacher John Prendergast has devoted his life to exploring the intersection and intermingling—indeed, the inherent inseparability—of the psychological and spiritual dimensions of being. In this profound, practical, and potentially life-changing meditation on the Heart in all its subtlety and complexity, he guides us on the journey home to our essential nature, with meditations and inquiry that lead us into and through our trauma and pain to our deepest inner knowing. If you read only one book on the spiritual journey this year, let it be this one!"

STEPHAN BODIAN
psychotherapist, spiritual teacher, and author
of *Wake Up Now* and *Beyond Mindfulness*

THE
DEEP
HEART

THE
DEEP
HEART

OUR PORTAL
TO PRESENCE

John J. Prendergast, PhD

sounds true
BOULDER, COLORADO

Sounds True
Boulder, CO 80306

This book is not intended as a substitute for the medical recommendations of
physicians, mental health professionals, or other health-care providers. Rather,
it is intended to offer information to help the reader cooperate with physicians,
mental health professionals, and health-care providers in a mutual quest for
optimal well-being. We advise readers to carefully review and understand
the ideas presented and to seek the advice of a qualified professional before
attempting to use them.

Published 2019

Cover design by Tara DeAngelis
Book design by Beth Skelley

Printed in Canada

Library of Congress Cataloging-in-Publication Data

Names: Prendergast, John J., 1950- author.
Title: The deep heart : our portal to presence / John J. Prendergast, PhD.
Description: Boulder, CO : Sounds True, [2019] | Includes bibliographical
   references.
Identifiers: LCCN 2019013298 | ISBN 9781683642527 (pbk.)
Subjects: LCSH: Self. | Self-realization. | Spiritual life.
Classification: LCC BF697 .P69486 2019 | DDC 158.1—dc23
LC record available at https://lccn.loc.gov/2019013298

eBook ISBN: 978-1-68364-318-0

10 9 8 7 6 5 4 3 2 1

To the light of awareness, Heart-Wisdom, our inner teacher

CONTENTS

Foreword by Adyashanti   ix

Introduction   1

1   The Pilgrimage from Head to Heart   9

2   The Wave and the Ocean
     The Multidimensional Heart   19

3   Meditation   33

4   Meditative Inquiry   45

5   The Body as Vibration and Space   55

6   Stepping Back From, Into, and Through Experience   63

7   Heartfelt Inquiry into Core Beliefs   77

8   Not Knowing and the Awakening of the Deep Heart   91

9   The Great Heart Holds the Human Heart   107

10   Is It Safe to Shine?   123

11   What about the Gut, or Hara?   131

12   The Heart in Relationship I
      Love, Lack, and Fullness   149

13   The Heart in Relationship II
      *Connection, Aloneness, Self-Judgment
      and Acceptance, and Listening*   159

14   Conclusion
      Coming Home to the Deep Heart   173

      Notes   179

      Additional Resources   185

      Acknowledgments   187

      About the Author   189

FOREWORD

AMONGST ALL OF the existential angst of modern life there is a blossoming of spirit arising within the collective psyche of humanity. As the modern mind feels increasingly adrift and unmoored from its rootedness in being, a quiet flame of spiritual presence is making its way through the forest of confusion. New voices and spiritual orientations are coming into being as spirit breaks out of the confines of its old structures, seeking expression and embodiment not only in religious institutions but in the embodied hearts of ordinary human beings. Such collective transitions are always somewhat chaotic, even dangerous, but they are also times of renewal and rebirth for those who will listen to the quiet and heartfelt voice of the spiritual presence within themselves.

To navigate the spirit of the modern psyche is no small matter. We need guides who at once have their feet firmly rooted in the ground and wisdom of our spiritual ancestors, while also embodying a deep understanding of the modern human condition. For the call of spirit today is to both awaken to our true spiritual identity and to embody that awakened consciousness in our humanity and daily lives. It takes an integrated and unified psyche to embody the wisdom and beauty of awakened consciousness. We are all called to be spiritually awake *and* whole human beings, not only for ourselves but for the sake and welfare of all sentient beings.

The Deep Heart is what I call a living book, that rare gem of a book that is alive with the presence of its author. Such presence and aliveness are as important of a teaching as the words on the page, for they convey the living reality of spirit through directly evoking it in the reader. So as you read through this wonderful and wise book, dedicate a little part of your attention to noticing the felt presence of the words themselves, and to listening to the silence between them. In that silence, you will feel within yourself the living reality the words point to. A book like *The Deep Heart* should be *felt* and *experienced* as much as it should be read.

As for the words on the page, they are expressions of John's many years of exploration of the human spirit *and* psyche, as well as a means to communicate the depth and breadth of his spiritual realization. Our true nature seeks to awaken from limiting identifications, but it seeks also to literally embody our deepest realizations throughout the entire mind and body. It is here where John's spiritual and psychological wisdom shines most brightly, for *The Deep Heart* is a book that unites the dimensions of heaven and earth within each of us.

The innate spiritual instinct within us all is circular. It seeks to awaken to the gods, but it is a surprise to find that the gods (within us) seek to become embodied human beings. Only when we realize our timeless divinity, and our divinity realizes its humanity, does the spirit come to rest in its wholeness.

The word *redemption* comes to mind. It means to return, or be returned, to one's natural condition of wholeness. *The Deep Heart* is a book that for all of its depth of wisdom and spiritual guidance is also a redemptive presence. It is a constant reminder to awaken to your true nature of presence and wholeness, to live it in your humanity, and in your heart, and in the way that you relate to all of life. And it is a reminder that each and every one of us has the capacity to be a redemptive presence in the world.

We can each be a part of what the world is trying to become. And that is no small matter, nor is it metaphor. It is the living reality of the deeper domain of the human psyche. The stakes are high, the responsibility profound, and the heart of humanity is at stake. So dive into *The Deep Heart* and renew your spirit with the living words of an important spiritual voice. And as you read through this book of wisdom, you might just sense John's quiet presence inviting and evoking an awakening to what you have never lost.

Adyashanti

INTRODUCTION

WITH THIS BOOK I invite you to look beneath the cover of your conditioned identity and take a deep dive into the heart of who you really are—your true nature. There is nothing more important to do, to feel, or to understand as a human being. Knowingly or unknowingly you have been searching for this your entire life. Like a beggar who has been sitting on a box of gold, the treasure lies radiant and intact in the very core of your being. You are fully equipped to discover it, regardless of your background and conditioning. You just need to look in the right direction with open eyes.

We all have a sacred calling that has very little to do with what we accomplish in this world. It is the calling *of* the sacred—the quiet pull of an implicit wholeness within each of us that awaits our conscious recognition. As this recognition unfolds, our relationship to life changes. Increasingly we find ourselves open to life as it is—and creative in our response.

Discovering the heart of who we really are is the essential human quest. This discovery changes our life and the lives of those around us. Our life increasingly becomes an offering—an upwelling and outpouring. No matter how our outer life changes—and it most certainly will—an inner light will spontaneously radiate out for the benefit of all beings.

As we attune with the heart, our approach to life reverses. Instead of feeling empty, agitated, and disconnected, we discover an inner fullness, peace, and sense of seamlessness. Instead of imagining that we are either a deflated or inflated, unworthy separate-self, we discover that we are a unique expression of a greater loving whole. Rather than anxiously willing our way through or avoiding life, we feel ourselves trusting and following an underlying flow of intelligence and love.

Instead of being whipped around by fears and desires, we feel a growing inner stability and sense of spaciousness, no matter what is happening. Rather than feeling like a lonely wanderer in a desolate landscape, a stranger in a strange land, we find our self at home wherever we are. The heart area is the portal, par excellence, for this discovery. This is my work and great love. I would like to share it with you.

A Window into the Deep Heart

For almost four decades, I have worked as a depth psychotherapist and more recently as a spiritual teacher. These roles have allowed me an unusual window into the hearts of my clients and students—into their most painful emotional wounds as well as their essential radiance of being.

I had little conscious knowledge of this territory when I first began this exploration. I was drawn to this work in my twenties with mixed motives. I had already been meditating for years and instructing others how to do so, but I found that I often felt anxious in social situations, despite the tranquility I experienced during meditation. I had relatively little insight about what was beneath the surface of my conscious mind other than a profound silence I could tap into while meditating. I knew that I wanted to face myself more directly, to be of service to others, and also to make a viable living. Beneath all of these motives there was a powerful underground current that I now recognize as a love for the truth and a relentless call to know myself.

Within a two-year period in my midtwenties, I went from a six-month meditation retreat in the Swiss Alps to law school, then to an ashram in South India, and finally to an unaccredited, alternative graduate school in San Francisco. Looking back, I can imagine that my parents experienced a kind of whiplash trying to keep up with my bewildering change of directions. Fortunately, they kept their doubts and anxieties to themselves (bless their hearts), as I was on my hands and knees feeling my way in the dark toward my inner calling.

Over the next fifteen years, I became a licensed psychotherapist while also immersing myself in meditation and self-inquiry. My primary teacher at the time was Jean Klein, a European master of Advaita

Vedanta that was strongly seasoned with Tantric Shaivism. I had met and immediately connected with Jean (pronounced with a soft *j* as they do in France) five years into my graduate training. During this period, I was driven by a curiosity to understand how psychology and spirituality intersected, but after several years of exploring both domains, I discovered that the apparent division between them was only in my mind. I realized that all thoughts, feelings, and sensations were expressions of consciousness, and I couldn't find any human experience that was not essentially spiritual. During this time, I also began to train and supervise masters' level counseling students at the California Institute of Integral Studies (CIIS) in San Francisco.

Jean Klein passed away in 1998. Three years later (and quite unexpectedly), I began to study with my second primary teacher, Adyashanti. Being with Adya catalyzed a number of profound openings that I will describe later in this book with the hope that they may help you find your way through similar terrain. I feel incredibly grateful for Adya's presence, teachings, and highly attuned individual attention. The gifts of these teachers illustrate the critical role that a genuine teacher can play in the unfolding process of self-recognition. I strongly doubt that my own understanding would have emerged without both Jean's and Adya's help.

I began to share my understanding in two self-inquiry groups and colead residential retreats for psychotherapists with my friend and colleague Dorothy Hunt, who had been invited by Adya to teach a few years earlier. After several years, Dorothy, with Adya's assent, invited me to do the same. Although I did not seek this role, it is one that I have grown into.

As my understanding continues to develop, both through teaching and a natural process of unfolding, I can often sense an essential dimension of being within my clients and students and help them attune with it. In my experience, most psychotherapists rarely contact this level or, if they do, often fail to recognize its significance. As a result, they confine their clients to a level of healing and integration that overlooks or misunderstands the most liberating resource in the core of their client's being. That said, I believe that there is substantial value to conventional psychological healing work, and I strongly support the critically important service that mature, kind, and relatively clear psychotherapists offer to their clients. Their dedicated work in the basement of the psyche can help set the stage for a spiritual realization to unfold.

Conversely, spiritual teachers who are emotionally immature and lack empathy will fail to recognize important dimensions of their students' hearts. This oversight can lead to teachings that are dry and abstract—cognitively brilliant and profound, but emotionally disconnected or poorly attuned. Following their teachers' lead, students can avoid being with vulnerable feelings such as shame, fear, doubt, or rage, and then continue to be ambushed by them, particularly in intimate relationships. Their spiritual practices will also be obstructed by unresolved emotional material. This phenomena, known as spiritual bypassing, is extremely common in spiritual circles.[1]

Our sense of meaning springs from the heart, as does our sense of oneness or communion with the whole of life.

The capacity for teachers to sense and share on an essential level with their students is a function of resonance or mutual attunement. We recognize in others what we sense in ourselves. When this attunement happens, we enjoy a shared experience of communion. While this type of meeting does not belong to anyone, there is no greater intimacy. When the heart has awakened, reality meets itself in an utterly simple, spacious, and loving way. It's a joy and a blessing when this unfolds between people. It's as if one is both a beautiful flower and an admiring gardener at the same time.

The Heart as a Portal

In one of my previous books, *In Touch: How to Tune In to the Inner Guidance of Your Body and Trust Yourself,* I described four subtle somatic markers that commonly arise as people get in touch with their inner knowing: openheartedness, spaciousness, groundedness, and a vibrant alignment and aliveness. These subtle markers are facets or essential qualities of our true nature. They are also portals—primary entry points leading to the essential. If you explore any of these portals, they will lead you to the same source. For instance, if you fully investigate the sense of the ground, you will discover a nonlocalized "groundless ground" that has a loving tone to it. So, too, when you let go into the deepest dimension of the heart—what I call the Great Heart—you can feel yourself at one with the ground of being. In this way, the portals of the ground and the heart beautifully converge in the same nonplace of our true nature.

This book builds on this earlier work by homing in on the heart. The heart area is central to human experience. It is where we feel most affected and touched, both emotionally and spiritually. Our sense of meaning springs from the heart, as does our sense of oneness or communion with the whole of life.

This does not diminish other ways of sensing our true nature. The whole body participates in the unfolding of inner knowing whether or not we are consciously aware of it. Some people may never explicitly sense the heart area or the interior of their body at all and still profoundly realize who they really are. Others will have easier access to different facets of inner knowing than the heart area. It is important to realize that there is not one right way for this understanding to emerge. Nonetheless, the heart area seems to be the most common, central, and easily accessible portal to true nature for most people. Accordingly, it deserves a book of its own.

*Whether we realize it or not, the heart is what
we most carefully guard and most want to open.*

The awakening of the heart is supported by a clear mind and a sense of inner stability. For example, we need to be able to unhook or disidentify from our core limiting stories in order for our attention to drop into the heart. This takes substantial clarity. Further, we need to feel a core sense of safety in order to keep our heart open.

This requires intimacy with the region of the belly (or hara) that governs, among other things, our instinct to survive. These central facets of our experience—what we could call the head, heart, and hara—work together as a team, supporting one another. Each has a critical role to play in the discovery of our true nature.

The heart area is where we feel most intimately touched by kindness, gratitude, and appreciation. It is where we feel most loving and loved. It is where we point when we refer to ourselves and where we feel the full poignancy of our human existence, richly flavored by both joy and grief. It is where and how we know ourselves and others most intimately. It is where we simply *are*, free of any definition. And it is where we move from when we are most at ease and in touch with ourselves. When the heart has awakened, we are intimate with all things.

Conversely, the heart is also where we feel most emotionally wounded by the words and acts of others, especially when we struggle with our own sense of worth. It is where we feel the impact of our harshest self-judgments and where we feel most hurt by the judgments of others. When we find it difficult to accept and love ourselves, our heart feels numb or disturbed. It is where we loathe and reject ourselves, it is where we are least kind to ourselves and others, and it is one of the primary centers of shame. It is where we feel brokenhearted when we have lost someone dear to us. It is the seat of despair, and it is where we feel most alone, empty, alienated, and disconnected.

It takes incredible courage to open our heart. The French word for heart is *coeur* (from the Latin *cor*)—the root of the word *courage*—and it takes enormous courage to explore the depths of the heart. We are sometimes more willing to risk physical danger than to open our heart to another and risk emotional wounding or the loss of what we take to be our self. Whether we realize it or not, the heart is what we most carefully guard and most want to open. I welcome you in this courageous exploration into your essential nature.

Getting Started

Take your time as you read this book. There's no need to rush. Slow down when something touches you; tune in to anything that resonates.

Question. Ponder. One of the main purposes of this book is to awaken your inner teacher. For this to happen, you need to listen to your heart wisdom—your deepest knowing.

While I do some conceptual mapping, this book is not a theoretical treatise; it is an experiential guide. Insight needs to be coupled with direct experience. Therefore, I have included a number of guided meditations and inquiries. These may be the most important parts of this book. I strongly recommend that you record these exercises on your smartphone in your own voice, leaving long periods of silence between the given steps. The practices are quite potent if you give yourself to them whole-heartedly. Try them a number of times.

In the opening chapter, I frame this exploration as a spiritual pilgrimage from the head to the heart, introducing several essential questions and the phenomenon of heart wisdom. In chapter 2, I offer a preliminary mapping of the multidimensional heart using the metaphor of the wave and the ocean to discuss ego, soul, and Self (or no-self). I also present the apparent paradox that we are both wounded and whole. Chapter 3 explores meditation and accents the importance of our clarity of intention and quality of attention. I differentiate between two kinds of meditation and offer a way to rest in (and as) awareness.

In chapter 4, I present a form of meditative inquiry that I have refined over many years. I also describe a partnered form of meditative inquiry, which brings a powerful interpersonal dimension to this normally solitary practice. Chapter 5 introduces the idea and experience of a subtle energy body—the body of vibration and space—and offers two long meditations to help attune with it. In chapter 6, I discuss skillful ways to be with our experience—stepping back from or into and through it. These complementary means correspond with transcendent and immanent approaches to life. I also disclose key principles and practices that I use in my one-on-one and group work.

Chapter 7 deals with the central role of core limiting beliefs and offers a clear and powerful way to recognize and see through them, whereas chapter 8 emphasizes the importance of not knowing with the ordinary mind as a door to an essential way of knowing. I describe subtle dimensions of the heart area as well as important openings in my own spiritual journey. In chapter 9, I then discuss how the Great Heart holds the vulnerable human heart and offer a guided meditation to feel held and explore the impacts of developmental trauma. I also describe ways to be with our conditioned wounding that accent the potential for our wounds to become portals to essential feelings and our true nature.

Chapter 10 explores whether it is now safe for the heart to safely shine. I describe how consciously or subconsciously we learn to guard our heart as children and then carry these patterns into our adult life. I present two cases from my mentoring work to illustrate what happens when we discover a dimension of the heart that does not need protection. Chapter 11 deals with the gut (or hara), which, when illumined, provides a foundation for the human heart to safely remain open. I discuss the themes of survival, sex, and power in detail and offer a meditation on the hara.

In chapters 12 and 13, I explore how the Deep Heart impacts our way of relating with others. You'll also find reflections on (and suggested meditative inquiries into) the themes of unconditional love, lack, connection, aloneness, judging, acceptance, soulful relating, and deep listening. Chapter 14, the conclusion, unpacks a beautiful aphorism by Adyashanti about the three stages of the spiritual journey. The final chapter of this book is the one you will author with your own life.

I welcome you to journey into the depths of your heart, carefully investigate who you have taken yourself to be, and discover the radiant presence that you are and always have been.

~ *One* ~

THE PILGRIMAGE
FROM HEAD TO HEART

In the room of lovers
I can see with closed eyes
the beauty that dances.

RUMI, "My Burning Heart,"
translated by Deepak Chopra and Fereydoun Kia

THERE IS A LIGHT in the core of our being that calls us home—one
that can only be seen with closed eyes. We can feel it as a radiance in
the center of our chest. This light of loving awareness is always here,
regardless of our conditioning. It does not matter how many dark
paths we have traveled or how many wounds we have inflicted or sustained as we have unknowingly stumbled toward this inner radiance. It
does not matter how long we have sleepwalked, seduced by our desires
and fears. This call persists until it is answered, until we surrender to
who we really are. When we do, we feel ourselves at home wherever
we are. A hidden beauty reveals itself in our ordinary life. As the true
nature of our Deep Heart is unveiled, we feel increasingly grateful for
no reason—grateful to simply be.

Rumi discovered this truth eight hundred years ago, as have ordinary people like you and me. It is the call from the depths of every
human heart. It is the call from your heart as you read these words
and something within you stirs in recognition. Rightly understood,

everything that happens invites us to recognize this heart-oriented way of being, knowing, and feeling.

The Inner Pilgrimage

You have heard of pilgrimages and perhaps been on one yourself, such as the famed Camino de Santiago that winds through Europe and ends at a Catholic cathedral near the Atlantic coast in Spain. For millennia, people have walked long distances in India to visit holy shrines or sacred mountains, such as Mount Kailash in the Himalayas or Arunachala in the south where the renowned twentieth-century sage Ramana Maharshi was drawn when he was sixteen and where he spent the rest of his life. Devout Muslims try to visit Mecca at least once in their lives. There are secular versions, as well, such as the pristine John Muir Trail in the high Sierras in California or the Appalachian Trail on the East Coast of the United States.

Whether our pilgrimages are religious or secular, they spring from the same source and ultimately have the same destination. They are archetypal in nature, arising from the depths of the human psyche. These journeys are attempts to return to wholeness—to recover our innocence, openheartedness, and inherent knowing. They are journeys toward the Deep Heart.

What is the most important thing in this brief life?
What is most real and true?

As powerful as these outer pilgrimages may be, the essential pilgrimage is inner. Rather than taking place over long distances and difficult terrain, *the inner pilgrimage is the abiding shift of attention from the forehead to the heart area.* Our attention is usually caught in the judging mind and identified with imprisoning stories and images. As a result, we feel vaguely located in our forehead or behind our eyes. Yet our true home is the Deep Heart—loving awareness, the very center of our being. The direction of our journey is not forward but backward, a falling back and letting go. This inner pilgrimage is a profound surrender into a different way of knowing, feeling, and being. It requires an attunement to and trust in something in the core of our being that is as compelling as it is invisible.

This inner pilgrimage almost always involves both understanding and some effort, at least at first. Spurred by suffering and drawn by an inner sense that there is something truer within us, we begin an inner search. We start to examine our direct experience more carefully and to question our commonsense assumptions about reality. Existential questions arise: *Who or what am I, really? What do I most value and care about? What is the most important thing in this brief life? What is most real and true?*

Along the way, we begin to realize that what we have thought was true is not. Increasingly we see that we *don't* really know who we are. The familiar scaffolding of personal identity becomes shaky. Our metaphoric nametags—who we thought we were—become scuffed and faded. Am I only this identity that I have constructed or this role that I play? What if these beliefs that I have clung to so tenaciously are not true? Perhaps I am not this unworthy person, essentially lacking or flawed, that I have subconsciously believed and felt myself to be? What if I am not actually a separate-self, cut off and alienated from everyone and everything (as most people seem to think and feel)? What if *all* of these identities are illusory, no more real than the characters in last night's dream?

We begin to realize that we are suffering from a case of mis-taken identity. In other words, we see that we have taken ourselves to be something that we are not. It is as if we are actors in a movie who have forgotten who we are and instead believe that we are the character we are playing. Fine actors immerse themselves in their roles without becoming lost in them. Yes, we do need to play our roles, most of which are natural and useful, yet we are neither defined by nor confined to them. For example, we may play the role of being a woman or a man, mother or father, American or Netherlander, Christian or Buddhist, conservative or progressive, worthy or unworthy, yet these social and psychological roles come and go. Who are we prior to our various social roles and psychological identities?

I recently offered an online session for hundreds of personal coaches who were interested in working from presence—that is, the conscious awareness of their being. After leading a guided meditation and giving a short talk, I had them break into twosomes with partners they had never met and to take turns posing the following question to one another: *Who are you, really?* I invited them to innocently listen to the question, take their time, not go to their mind for an answer, and then spontaneously respond. They broke away to work with this question and came together a few minutes later. As we debriefed, many were astonished at what this simple inquiry led to. They experienced their familiar identities quickly falling away and the emergence of a heartfelt clarity and joy.

Equally interesting, even though these coaches were scattered across the globe, the whole group shared a palpable sense of intimacy. They only needed to be willing to honestly explore, pose the right question, and enter into a different way of listening. As a result, a profound inner dialogue quickly unfolded that was followed by a contagious sense of well-being. It was striking to see and feel how resonant this discovery was for so many people who had never met before. They had quickly tapped into their shared ground by sincerely questioning their commonsense identities. Rather than being unnerved, they were delighted by what they discovered within themselves and between themselves and others—a vibrant communion.

It is a huge relief to see and feel that we are not who,
where, or when we have taken our self to be.

There is so much that we take for granted that isn't really true. For example, we think that we are a separate-inside-self living within a separate-outside-world.[1] In other words, we think we are inside this body somewhere, although when we carefully look, we can't locate exactly where. How often have you actually questioned this assumption? Alan Watts, the self-described philosophical entertainer, wrote, "The prevalent sensation of oneself as a separate ego enclosed in a bag of skin is a hallucination."[2] Are we really separate and divided from the whole of life?

This particular question is a variation of a classic form of self-inquiry. *Where* exactly are you? If you sit with this question with an open mind, you will be surprised by what you discover. If you are honest and quietly observant, it becomes increasingly difficult to find the boundary between an inner self and an outer world. Indeed, you may discover that rather than being in the world, the world is in you—as open, infinite awareness, not as the little *me*.

For that matter: *When* exactly are you? We usually take for granted that we are moving on a timeline from the past to the future, like an inchworm working its way along a marked ruler. Yet if we reflect on our actual experience, we realize that we have never experienced the past other than in our thinking. The so-called past is always a memory in present time. Nor have we experienced the future other than in our imagination—again only in present time. When we consult our direct experience, we realize that the past and future are only concepts. Even more surprisingly, when we try to find the so-called now, we can't. Now, in fact, is timeless. So when are we? It is hard to say, isn't it? Is it okay to know that we are essentially a timeless being? Can we still pay the bills on time with the revelation that we are, in truth, free from time?

If we are scrupulously honest, we discover that we actually don't know what we are, where we are, or when we are. This discovery is unsettling and profoundly liberating. Once we get over the initial shock, it is a huge relief to see and feel that *we are not who, where, or when we have taken our self to be*. The truth is that we don't know and can't know any of this—at least not with our ordinary strategic, goal-oriented mind.

We discover that we can rest in not knowing. This is not the same as being ignorant. We are not ignoring anything. In fact, we are facing an important truth—the limits of the conditioned mind. There is a great deal in life that we don't know, can't know, and perhaps most importantly, don't need to know. This insight frees attention to move from its temporary residence in the forehead to the depths of the heart area. Acknowledging that we *don't know* opens us to a different type of knowing.

Heart Wisdom, Homecoming, and Sacred Grief

Not knowing opens us to wisdom infused with love—to heart wisdom. An initial clarity unfolds into wise love. The sacred inner pilgrimage, unconsciously played out repeatedly in painful outer scenarios, finds its fruition with this discovery. As we know this for ourselves, we feel increasingly at home and free.

The curious thing is that once we find ourselves at home, it feels strangely familiar, as if we have known it all along. We have. We lived here once before as little children, albeit unknowingly. When we were very young, we were in our natural innocence and wholeness, but without consciously realizing it. It is obvious when we observe toddlers delightfully exploring their world or when we look into the transparent, open pools of their eyes. This innocent way of being was once true for each of us. We once experienced a simple joy, wonder, and beauty. Do you remember a time when you were "trailing clouds of glory" as Wordsworth wrote? Do you have moments when this truth peeks out now?

We inevitably forget our native innocence as we grow, leaving it behind like buried treasure as we adapt and individuate. We turn away from our essence to face the world—above all the world of people. If we are lucky, our caretakers will be relatively stable and loving. Sometimes, however, they battle their own inner demons of trauma and unworthiness, and, as a result, they may be neglectful, poorly attuned, highly critical, or even abusive. When this is the case, we quickly learn to harden ourselves.

If we sense that we are not safe or loved, we instinctively shut down. The earlier this happens, the less conscious the process is. Very early on, few if any conscious thoughts are involved. We can sense and feel an unwelcoming environment before we are even capable of forming a belief. Gradually or suddenly, consciously or unconsciously, we close our heart and armor our body and mind, all to protect a native sensitivity that we do not consciously recognize or understand.

Even when we have a relatively benign upbringing, our brain and mind naturally develop to overshadow a more direct and intuitive way of being that we knew as young children. Our systems of education tend to reinforce this analytic mode since it is so useful for solving external problems. In addition, there are always shocks and losses along the way that we must somehow navigate—uprootings, divorces, illnesses, and deaths.

Recently, during a day-long retreat, I partnered with one of the retreatants to explore the question: *What is the true nature of your heart?* Once she relaxed and settled in, she reported an emerging sense of awe as she felt her heart area opening into "a vastness that includes everything." Later when we debriefed, she realized with gratitude that she had unknowingly sensed this innocent and open way of being as a small child.

The loss of innocence often passes unnoticed. We are usually too busy learning and adapting, and thus lose touch with what we leave behind. We carry this loss into our adulthood as a formless grief and sense of alienation. When we slow down and start to sense the heart area, we can sometimes feel a profound, hard-to-define loss that does not seem to be linked to a specific person or place. This is puzzling if we think of loss only in terms of losing a loved one. If we feel profoundly sad, it seems that we must have lost someone or something, even if we can't quite put our finger on who or what this might be. In fact, the lost beloved is the knowing and feeling of our Deep Heart.

I have often encountered this nameless grief among my clients and students who are undergoing a deep inner search. It took me awhile to recognize what it actually was, since it was not described in the conventional psychological literature. I now see this grief as existential and sacred. If we open to it and follow it all the way in, it leads us back to the treasure that we left behind. In this way our existential grief can guide us to a profound self-knowledge and abiding joy.

Until the Deep Heart awakens, we will believe and feel that
we are a separate-inside-self in a separate-outside-world.

Life does not end with the completion of this inner pilgrimage. As this essential search winds down, a new life begins. While the search for our true inner home ends with the awakening of the heart, the discovery of life continues to unfold and be expressed in surprisingly vibrant, creative, playful, and intimate ways. When we knowingly return to our native innocence, life opens up, and we are able to see "the beauty that dances" that Rumi alluded to in the opening epigraph. The death of our socially constructed, commonsense identity makes space for a profound renewal and discovery—a rebirth.

It's Not the Pump

When I write about the human heart, I am not referring to the physical pump on the left side of the chest, despite its interesting electromagnetic qualities. Rather, I mean the center of extraordinary sensitivity in the center of the chest that has infinite depth. It is a multidimensional center of being, knowing, and feeling. Our experience of it can range across a wide spectrum—from the gross, through the subtle, to the infinite. Our sense of self can accordingly vary from being highly constricted and exclusive to being infinitely expansive and inclusive. Likewise, our knowing can range from being densely veiled and distorted to being transparently clear. Further, our capacity to feel can range from being relatively numb to being exquisitely attuned and quietly joyful, or anywhere in between.

Our subjective experience of the heart varies enormously depending upon how intimate we are with it and, correspondingly, how separate we take ourselves to be from others. If we are distant and alienated from our Self, we will in turn experience this with others. For example, if on some level we are caught in a story of our unworthiness and the related feelings of shame and the fear of rejection, we feel split within ourselves and separate from others. To put it simply, our heart feels closed, so much so that we may not even know what an open heart feels like. Most of us have had at least episodes of thinking and feeling this way. If this state becomes chronic, we will feel that we are lacking or flawed in an uncaring or hostile universe. As a result, we suffer unnecessarily, radiating this suffering out to those around us.

Regardless of our level of personal self-esteem, until the Deep Heart awakens, we will believe and feel that we are a separate-inside-self in a separate-outside-world. Existential psychologists call this a self-world view. Most of us are identified with and trapped in such a view, at least to some degree. The extraordinarily good news is that we don't have to be.

I will discuss methods of investigation in subsequent chapters, but at this point I want to introduce you experientially to the domain of the heart simply by inviting you to shift your attention from the head to the heart area, via a centering breath, touch, and feeling. As you learn to pay attention to this area, your sensitivity will grow and a surprising depth will unfold. Doing so at first may feel like tending a garden with only a few budding plants or a hearth with a few glowing embers. It may take a little effort to focus your attention in this new direction. In time the process develops a momentum of its own and becomes effortless.

MEDITATION
Tending the Heart

Sit comfortably where you won't be disturbed for a few minutes, close your eyes, and take several deep, slow breaths. Then ask yourself, "Is there a problem right now? Is there anything that needs my attention right now that can't wait for a few minutes?" If there isn't (there almost never is), let your attention drop down to the center of your chest. Imagine that you can inhale into and exhale directly from the heart area. Put a hand over the center of your chest and think of someone or something that you love, appreciate, or feel grateful toward. Notice what you sense, and stay with your experience for another few minutes, allowing it to develop.

Bring your attention out and go about your day. Notice the shift in your sense of being and way of relating that happens afterward.

~

Two

THE WAVE AND THE OCEAN

The Multidimensional Heart

Blessed are the pure in heart, for they will see God.

JESUS, Matthew 5:8 (New International Version)

WHAT DO I mean by the Deep Heart? What is it, exactly, and what does it entail? I want to share a multidimensional map with you, one that I have distilled after years of exploration. This map of the heart is simple, subtle, and incomplete. It's also not completely original—others have described similar strata of the psyche.

We can access three broad levels of experience and identity in and through the heart area: ego, soul, and Self (or no-self). I will briefly introduce these levels here and touch on them in future chapters. Of course, any terrain is much more complex than a map could ever convey, and the two should never be confused. All maps, particularly inner ones, are limited. Their value lies in accurately pointing us in the right direction, no more. We must explore the territory for ourselves.

The classic metaphor of the wave and the ocean can help illuminate this three-layered map. Imagine a wave on the ocean, as well as the tip of the wave. Level one of our commonsense identity resembles this wave tip. It's our egoic identity as a separate-self. From this perspective, our life is brief, turbulent, and achingly separate. Despite our conscious attempts to stay busily distracted, on some level we always feel vulnerable and subtly groundless. We fear that a gust of wind could blow us apart like a piece of sea foam.

When we look out upon the world from this highly limited perspective, we can only see an endless expanse of separate wave tips that we must somehow navigate. We live in a world of separation, full of anxiety. We observe that these other wave tips, some familiar and beloved, eventually disappear, and we realize that a similar fate awaits us one day. From the viewpoint of a wave tip that can only see horizontally, the ocean—the substratum that all waves share in common—is invisible. There is only an unknown darkness beneath us—a terrifying abyss.

Further, as separate wave forms, we try to establish meaningful relationships with each other without risking abandonment, engulfment, or fragmentation. We try to avoid being left, becoming consumed, or going mad. Our interpersonal life is fraught with danger. Since the surface of this ocean is constantly in flux, everyone and everything comes and goes, arising and passing away. Despite our plans and best efforts, nothing happens exactly as we expect. There are plenty of unanticipated twists and turns, not to mention rude surprises. Few of us ever imagined that our lives would turn out as they have.

Ego

For the purpose of this book, I'm using the term *ego* to refer to our self-story and image, along with its related feelings and sensations. It is who most of us ordinarily think and feel that we are. I am not using the word to refer to a differentiated and unique sense of self or various "executive functions," such as the ability to remember, discern, or decide. There is a critically important distinction between being egocentric (self-centered and disconnected) and being individuated (differentiated). We can express ourselves differently without feeling an underlying sense of separation. In fact, our sense of having a shared ground liberates our distinctive expressions. Essential unity fosters healthy diversity.

Ego in Latin simply means "I." As we discover who we really are as infinite loving awareness, our sense of self or *I-ness* simplifies and clarifies. As we more fully recognize our pure subjectivity, we are content to be without any conscious or subconscious self-definition. We wear our costumes of social identity lightly and can discard them at a moment's notice. This in turn frees us to be much more spontaneous, unique, and truly creative in our expression. In this case, less really is more.

Exploring the Heartfelt Sense of "I"

Sit comfortably, close your eyes, and take a few deep, slow breaths. Feel the weight of your body held by whatever you are sitting upon. Then bring your attention to the center of your chest. Introduce the thought "I," repeating it sub-vocally several times: I . . . I . . . I . . . Let go of the thought and notice if there is a subtle sensation that arises in the heart area. Don't try to make anything happen, just innocently sense what comes. If a sensation does arise, follow it backward, tracing it to its source. If you discover stillness, silence, and a sense of vast, wakeful space, simply rest in this for as long as you like. Notice the impact of doing so as you go about your day.

~

This egoic level of identity is so commonplace, so normal, that we don't even consider it as a level. To question its reality—to see ego identity as a mental-emotional-somatic construct, a kind of virtual tunnel vision—just doesn't make sense. For most people, it's just how things are. We cannot see what we are lost within, no more than we can usually know we are in a dream while we are dreaming.

But just as we can learn to dream lucidly, we can also experience lucid waking. Having someone point out that our commonsense identity is a mind-construct is quite helpful. It's like having someone come up to you in a dream to remind you that you are dreaming. As an aside, during a lucid dream, I once tried to tell the other characters that they were dreaming, but no one was interested! The same seems to be largely true in the waking state.

We are not only this body.

Level one—ego identity—is all about location, ownership, and agency. It sounds like a business, doesn't it? Metaphorically speaking, some of us are relatively good "business" people who are able to navigate egoic life well enough to achieve some degree of security and happiness—at least until loss, disability, and death knock on our door so strongly that we can no longer ignore them. We say that such people are well-adjusted. There is merit to this way of being that we should not dismiss too quickly. Well-adjusted individuals, families, groups, and nations are a lot easier and more pleasant to live with than those who are not. They start fewer wars and generally create a more peaceful outer life for themselves and others. Having a relatively coherent and resilient sense of self, even if it remains on an egoic level, is an asset.

On the egoic level, when we say "I," "me," or "mine," we mean the one who apparently is located inside this body: "I'm in here somewhere—don't ask me exactly where." We feel that we are localized in space and time. We also believe that we are the exclusive owner of this limited rental space of the body, for example, "It's *mine*." We are also apparently the one to whom body-related thoughts and feelings are referring: "*My* thoughts and feelings." If you observe your thoughts and feelings for a little while, you will notice that most of them refer directly or indirectly to the actions, needs, desires, and fears of your body or your self-image, which is also fundamentally body-based. You will also notice that these thoughts are extremely repetitive and often fearful.

We call these thoughts and feelings self-referential or self-centered because we believe, quite understandably, that we are limited to this one specific body that we apparently inhabit. Heart wisdom will eventually reveal that, although we *are* this body along with its related thoughts, feelings, and sensations, we are also unimaginably more. From some classic nondual teachings we initially learn that we are *not* this body, I find it more accurate to say that we are *not only* this body. It's a more inclusive formulation and one that is less likely to foster dissociation.

This apparently separate "me" also believes that it is an independent agent either fully in charge of its life or completely powerless to do anything about it. The separate-self believes that it is the successful or unsuccessful doer. There is either an inflated or collapsed sense of the personal will that corresponds to being either an over- or underachiever.

In the same way that our sense of location and ownership opens up as we discover our true nature, so too does our sense of agency. We discover a will that is not self-serving. This transpersonal will is *willing* rather than *willful*. It carries much greater power than the personal will. Gandhi called this "truth-power" (satyagraha) because it is connected to a fundamental truth or reality.

There is a way of acting that is neither aggressive nor passive. Action can spontaneously, rather than impulsively, spring from a source that is prior to the commonsense polarity of will. As attention shifts to the heart area, we are able to act in an increasingly responsive and responsible way without feeling that we are the doer. We experience that doing is happening, but no one is doing; choices are made, but no one is choosing.

Finally, the egoic level involves so-called self-consciousness. We actually feel self-conscious when we are concerned about what *others* think and feel about us: "Do you think I am okay or doing it right?" When we are consumed by this doubt, we feel anxious and awkward. Self-consciousness is rooted in our social consciousness—by how much our sense of self is shaped by our family and the larger culture. So-called self-consciousness is typically *others*-consciousness—that is, what we imagine others think and feel about us. It is an important step to recognize that our thoughts about others' views of us are mostly our projections of what we think and feel about ourselves. Deep self-awareness and self-acceptance undermine this tendency to project onto or judge others. As we stop judging ourselves, we stop judging others. Everyone benefits.

Plumbing the depths of the psyche is like an archeological dig. We discover older material the further we dig down. Ego-identity starts early and runs deeply in the psyche. Most children begin to recognize their physical images in a mirror and refer to themselves as "I" by age two. Interestingly, this capacity for mirror-recognition is also shared by all the great apes, Asian elephants, bottlenose dolphins, orcas, and even "bird-brained" European magpies.[1] Although they are unable to express it in formal language, it is likely that at least some of our fellow creatures share some sense of subjectivity.

When we enter into a process of self-examination, either on our own or with the help of a teacher or therapist, we uncover more superficial levels of defense and identity. As the process evolves, earlier strata and occasional "fossils"—formations of simpler thoughts and feelings from earlier psychological periods—emerge. We find evidence of T-Rexes or Pterodactyls—buried rage or shame—remains from an earlier, difficult era of psychological conditioning. People will often describe this material as both old and young—old since it seems like it has been with them for their whole life and young because it happened when they were quite young.

This is the realm of the inner child. There are, in fact, distinctly childish and childlike parts of the psyche that have their own voices, beliefs, and feelings. Some are highly compartmentalized and largely out of view of the conscious mind. They seem to live in their own worlds, frozen in time. These semi- and subconscious parts carry much of our early programming, which turns out to be mostly misprogramming.

This happens as we try to make sense out of challenging or distorted family environments with limited understanding, tools, and experience. We are easily confused. As children it can feel as if we woke up in the middle of a battlefield or wasteland without a map or clue as to what is happening around us. If we are attacked or neglected, we naturally tend to conclude that something must be wrong or missing with us. A lot of conventional psychotherapy works one way or another to uncover and rework this early programming. In some cases, we need to make sense out of our early experiences to form what psychologists call a "coherent narrative." A clear and kind story about ourselves can be quite helpful along the way, as long as we don't hold it too tightly.

These childlike parts are also closely connected to a native innocence and essential qualities of being. These parts live on the borders of the soul. As we learn to embrace these young parts—a process that often takes some time, understanding, and kindness—we discover that these apparent troublemakers are also unknowing gift-bearers. Some who wear tattered rags carry jewels in their hidden pockets. Rage disguises an inherent power, shame carries innocence in its core, and terror offers a direct path to fearlessness. Our shadows bear essential radiance.

Soul

The soul level is an intermediary dimension between ego and Self. This level is often denied or dismissed by rationally oriented psychologists who have never contacted it experientially. It's also often overlooked by those spiritual teachers who accent the transcendent and impersonal. It is a subtle, archetypal level explored by Jungians, students of shamanism, purpose guides, and people interested in unusual states of consciousness. Transpersonal psychology has become largely fixated on the soul for decades. New Agers also tend to gravitate here, fascinated by the possibility of cultivating subtle powers of the mind to gain wealth, health, or status via the law of attraction.

When we are open and attuned to this level, we feel ourselves moving more intuitively in harmony with a greater flow.

In my experience, when people are in touch with this soulful level of experience, a subtle jewel-like point at the back of the heart area opens and lights up. A signature vibration emerges—a particular blend of tones and colors (poetically speaking) that is unique to each individual. This illumination corresponds with the specific archetypes we express—healer, teacher, leader, artist, nurturer, explorer, and warrior (or some blend of these). These roles express essential qualities of being such as love, wisdom, courage, and beauty. When we experience someone who clearly expresses these qualities, we are moved and say that our "soul"—this deep level of the heart—is touched.

It's easy to identify with the soul level because it is so compelling. However, if we claim these archetypal energies and qualities as our own, our self-importance tends to inflate, and we can become "possessed" by the archetype, believing that we are somehow God's special gift to humanity. The operative word is *special*. I once experienced this state of inflation during my last trip to India in 1988. As I sat in my hotel room in Bangalore (Bengaluru), I began to feel that I was on a divine mission. Even though I had just become an adjunct faculty member at the California Institute of Integral Studies, I was sure that I would soon become president of the institute, dazzling people with my brilliant leadership and spiritual insight. Fortunately, this delusion passed within a day.

If this trance is not broken, the results can be personally and collectively dangerous. We may believe that we are on a sacred mission as the divinely chosen one—the prophet or savior—and take ourselves and our naïve followers off a cliff. This happens frequently with religious and political cults that have charismatic leaders. More commonly, we may feel arrogant and superior to others, and subtly pull to be recognized and admired. This can happen to emotionally immature nondual teachers who take themselves as special "no ones." We are all subject to this potential seduction. Self-honesty and vulnerability help us avoid this trap.

Returning to our metaphor of the wave and the ocean, the soul level is where the wave meets the ocean. We can sense subtler, deeper currents of movement here that guide us toward resonant friendships, intimate partnerships, authentic spiritual teachers and teachings, and creative careers. When we are open and attuned to this level, we feel ourselves moving more intuitively in harmony with a greater flow. We can sense this transitional level between the separate-self and unbounded awareness as a portal at the very back of the heart area.

Self or No-Self: The Great Heart

The deepest dimension—level three: the Self or no-self—is unbounded and infinite, unlike any worldly ocean that has a limit, no matter how vast. I call this the Great or Universal Heart. Our oceanic metaphor dissolves here, unable to contain what it points to. Some Buddhists might call this domain "no-self" in order to avoid making it into a subtle object. It seems to me that the concepts of Self and no-self point to the same direct realization. To call this reality the "Self" accents the every-thingness or fullness of our true nature; to call it "no-self" accents its no-thingness or emptiness—both are true depending upon whether we look from the perspective of love or wisdom. As Nisargadatta Maharaj famously said, "Love says that I am everything. Wisdom says that I am nothing. Between the two, my life flows."[2]

When we consciously recognize the Self or no-self on the level of the mind—what we can call a *mental* awakening—we experience a sense of infinite spaciousness and inner freedom. There is a profound clarity that who we really are is not bound by any story, image, or thought. When we consciously recognize the Self on the level of the heart—an *emotional* awakening—there is a profound sense of fullness and intimacy. We know and feel that we are innately whole and that everyone and everything is also made up of the same infinite loving awareness. When we consciously recognize the Self on the level of the gut or hara—an *instinctual* awakening—we experience a profound sense of existential stability, a groundless ground.

In the same way that we can become identified with the ego or the soul levels, it is possible for the separate-self to identify with glimpses of the Self or no-self and to make it part of one's self-image. The separate-self will appropriate any experience for itself. This takes the form of thoughts such as *I am enlightened (and you are not)* accompanied by a sense of superiority and separation, the proverbial "stink of Zen."[3] We can become infatuated with our awakening experiences, continually recounting them to ourselves and others in order to subtly fortify an image of being a special spiritual somebody, forgetting that the recognition of our true nature is always moment to moment and that awakening does not belong to or refer to anyone. Awakening is never personal. Awareness awakens to itself.

In this model, the tip of an individual wave has its source in the ocean just as the little "me" has its roots in infinite awareness. It is the same awareness, either tightly contracted and densely veiled or infinitely expanded and transparently clear. When this is clearly seen and felt, every individual wave—every differentiated person—is recognized as an intimate and unique expression of the ocean.

In the end, whether formed or formless, it's all water. We are both the wave and the ocean. When we track the oceanic nature of the wave back to its source, we remember who we truly are. Discovering this wholeness shared by all beings allows the individual wave to fully express itself, and the wave is free to play. On a human level, we are freed to be our creative and quirky selves and to accept others just as they are.

Unveiling the Heart:
We Are Both Wounded and Whole

If this layered map of the heart is roughly accurate, how do we go about unveiling our deepest nature? Let's approach that question by noticing any commonsense assumptions embedded in it. Is there a separate doer who must try to do something? Is there actually something basically lacking or flawed within our self? Is there a special state to achieve that is separate from the awareness that we experience right now?

> *As human beings, we are always both*
> *essentially whole and relatively wounded.*

We generally assume that we must begin by slowly working our way through dense levels of conditioning before we can encounter what is essential. Fortunately, this is not the case. There are no preconditions for experiencing our true nature, the true nature that is always available as the background awareness to and core of every experience. It is here right now as you read this sentence. For this reason, we can have glimpses or profound openings at any moment—when we are extremely depressed (Eckhart Tolle and Byron Katie), staring at a moldy shag rug in an Oregon motel (Joel Morwood), or standing at a bus stop in Paris (Suzanne Segal).[4] It is important to keep an open mind about when and how an unveiling may happen because we never know when reality may break through and induce lucidity. The sun of awareness can pierce the fog of the conditioned mind at any moment.

Discovering that we are essentially whole does *not* mean that we are free of psychological conditioning. When Westerners first encountered the enlightenment teachings from the East, we often assumed that awakening to our true nature would also free us from all of our psychological issues. I naïvely thought this way. After all, wouldn't attaining unitive consciousness ensure a constant state of bliss and harmonious relationships? This seemed like a reasonable, if rare, possibility.

Reality quickly intruded as we discovered that gurus, avatars, rinpoches, rishis, and roshis, along with their Western senior students, often secretly and sometimes openly acted out their psychological baggage in the domains of sex, money, and power. This fact has resulted in a disillusioning but highly useful insight: spiritual realization does not necessarily translate into psychological maturity. We have discovered that these are semi-independent lines of development that may or may not converge. Their congruence seems to center around the issue of integrity—our willingness to be rigorously honest with our self and others.

As human beings, we are always both essentially whole and relatively wounded. It is simply a question of levels. Clearly, we can be developed on one level and immature on another. This condition depends upon where we put our attention and what we most care about. If we are more interested in feeling good and thinking better about ourselves, we will focus our attention on the egoic level. If we are fascinated with the soul-level, we will focus on experiencing archetypes, states, and essential qualities. And if we are interested in uncovering our true nature, we will give our heart to our inherent wholeness and nonseparateness. Attention to one level can be complementary to another, if we remain open-minded and openhearted.

I find that my mentoring and therapeutic work with students and clients spontaneously weaves between these levels, and smooth navigation between them calls for a certain fluency. Learning the languages of neighboring countries makes it much easier to cross their borders.

While we may glimpse our true nature regardless of our present circumstances or past psychological conditioning, these "peek" experiences are much more difficult to sustain without a relatively stable nervous system and sense of inner resilience. In fact, if we are psychologically shaky, dramatic and genuine spiritual openings can destabilize us. Solid psychological work may be necessary to support a preliminary stabilization of the body-mind. We may need to feel a certain degree of visceral trust in our self and others before we can sustain an openness to the groundless ground.

On the other hand, realizing that we are essentially whole is a huge relief from the self-improvement project. Recognizing that we are fundamentally well allows us to relax. An inner struggle winds down as we stop trying to manipulate ourselves and others. Recently a young man shared with me something that touched him at the end of a day-long retreat: "I discovered my native wholeness today. It really is true, isn't it? I am already whole as I am!" I could sense that his discovery came from the deepest level of his heart. As he spoke, I could feel that an essential and transformative insight was consciously vibrating in his core.

As we viscerally recognize our native wholeness, our relationship to our conditioned body-mind becomes increasingly less conditional. Rather than trying to rid ourselves of an uncomfortable experience—for instance, an emotional reaction or somatic contraction—we are drawn to be intimate with it, even if it never changes. This is similar to wanting to get to know someone without secretly trying to change them.

Our attention becomes innocent, affectionate, and curious. Just as people naturally open up when we approach them from this openness, our inner experience responds similarly. Every inner reaction or constriction is waiting to be met with understanding and kindness. Almost always, sooner or later, some shift spontaneously unfolds from such an open encounter. Sometimes these shifts happen without any conscious attention, and we can find ourselves feeling lighter and more at ease for no apparent reason. At these times we can sense that we are being benevolently worked on by some greater intelligence outside of our conscious awareness.

The heart unveils itself unexpectedly. We may start from an outer egoic level and gradually work our way in, navigating through layers of resistance and emotional pain before encountering the peaceful and expansive depths of the heart. This is certainly a common route. Conversely, we may start from a sense of our essential wholeness, if this is consciously accessible. Often attention spontaneously moves between these levels. There are no rules to this fluid process of unfolding.

Sometimes we can engage in this investigation by ourselves via silent meditation and self-inquiry, assisted by readings, online videos, and an occasional retreat. At other times we can truly benefit by working with an attuned teacher, therapist, or life coach, or by sharing honestly with a trusted partner or friend. If we keep others at a safe distance, we can easily avoid certain vulnerable issues, such as the fear of being rejected and abandoned. Conversely, we can also avoid facing the fear of aloneness by clinging to unhealthy relationships. There are an almost infinite number of ways to avoid or bypass being with our direct experience. After years of practice, we are experts at resisting.

~ *Three* ~

MEDITATION

When the meditator disappears, there is meditation.
JEAN KLEIN, *Yoga Journal*

DOES THE UNVEILING of the heart's true nature happen spontaneously or by conscious intent? These apparently distinct ways of opening are not really separate; they go hand in hand. Conscious intent, when it is fully attuned, is also an expression of an underlying spontaneous wisdom.

Unveilings can happen on their own, out of the blue, for no apparent reason. There may be a hidden process of inner maturation that precedes a sudden and sustained awakening. Ramana Maharshi's inspiration to simulate death and then discover his true nature as pure consciousness at age sixteen is a famous example.[1] These kinds of openings, however, are rare.

More commonly, we are humbled by intense suffering that causes something like an inner rope burn. Unbearable physical or emotional pain may force us to let go of our tight grip on who we think and feel we are. The loss of a loved one or our own life-threatening illness can catalyze a profound seeing through of conditioning. Thirty years ago, the death of my first wife, Linda, viscerally ripped through any remaining illusions I had that physical reality was stable and continuous, triggering a profound inquiry into emptiness and impermanence.

Similarly, on the other end of the experiential spectrum, we can be opened by unexpected beauty and awe. Once when I was backpacking in the Desolation Wilderness area west of Lake Tahoe in the Sierra Nevada Mountains, I stretched out on a slab of granite at dusk and watched a silvery full moon slowly rise over the eastern ridge as the golden sun was setting to the west. Observing these two luminous spheres, one coming as the other left, unexpectedly catalyzed an intense heart opening. I barely slept that night as I was filled with an immense gratitude for everyone I had loved or been loved by. Life has a way of bringing us to our knees and opening us up, especially when we are willing.

We can either voluntarily disrobe or be forcefully stripped. One way or another, we have to let go of our illusions, and it's much easier if we cooperate. To use a related metaphor, if we are immersed in a swift river, we can frantically try to grab onto passing branches and boulders, or we can relax and float downstream, trusting that something greater is holding us and that we are being taken where we need to go. This trust goes against our strongly conditioned reflex to try to control everything in order to survive.

Our willingness to let go is fueled by two complementary desires: first, to avoid suffering; second, to know the truth. We are both pushed and pulled toward an unveiling. The proportion of these fuels will vary from person to person. Each fuel has a compelling power.

In my case, I was motivated more by the desire for truth, which grew clearer over time. My upbringing was fairly benign, although certainly not without its challenges. Between the ages of ten and thirteen I would often drift into a reverie before falling asleep in which I sensed what felt like infinite space. At age seventeen after listening to a recording of Ravi Shankar playing the sitar, I was drawn to explore Indian culture and began to read about its yogis, saints, and sages, such as Yogananda and Sri Ramakrishna. At age twenty I tried mescaline and LSD one time each and had transcendent experiences. Shortly after this, I stopped experimenting with psychedelics, began a daily meditation practice, and was off and running on my spiritual search, attending a series of long meditation retreats and immersing myself in the teachings of Vedanta, which were derived from the Upanishads.

As my practice and understanding matured, I became less interested in feeling better, experiencing expansive states, or secretly becoming a saint (talk about an egoic project!), and more interested in knowing what is true. This clarified desire was further supported by Nisargadatta Maharaj (first through a lucid dream and then through reading his seminal *I Am That*) and then by my two main teachers, Jean Klein and Adyashanti. Looking back, none of this unveiling was personal, even though it seemed intensely so at the time.

As we let go into the current of truth, it gains momentum, and an increasingly intimate inner dialogue unfolds between our conditioned mind and our unconditioned nature. If you want to cooperate with this process (which I assume you do, having read this far), it is important to honestly examine your motives.

MEDITATIVE INQUIRY
What Do You Really Want?

Find a quiet, comfortable place where you won't be disturbed, close your eyes, and take a few deep breaths. Let your attention settle down and in, resting in the heart area. When you are ready, ask yourself: "What is it that I really want?" Let the question go. Don't go to your mind for an answer. Just wait, listen, sense, and feel. The response may come first as a sensation or as an image before it becomes a word. Or it may come first as a word or phrase.

Whatever comes, check for inner resonance. Does it ring true for you? Something usually lights up, enlivens, releases, or opens up in the body if you have touched an important, inner truth.

~

It is crucial to be honest with yourself. Usually we have mixed motives. I certainly did. Even as I was highly interested in discovering what is true, I was also looking for approval from others and wanting to survive. Social acceptance and physical safety are fundamental, closely intertwined desires, and we often need to play them out until we see through them. This usually takes time.

If you believe that your happiness depends upon finding the right partner or career, or upon accumulating wealth or power, you may need to explore these options in order to discover their limitations. Conceptual insight—knowing that happiness does not depend upon circumstances—is rarely enough. Your life experience is a vital curriculum, and there will be a number of opportunities to experience its fierce grace.

You may be able to speed up this process by asking yourself what you imagine you will gain if you acquire the objects or meet the goals you are seeking. As a thought experiment, complete some of the following sentences that resonate for you:

If I find the right partner, I will feel _____.

If I have children or grandchildren, I
will experience _____.

If I have enough good friends or belong to the
right community, I will feel _____.

If I have the right job or career, I will be _____.

If I have enough money and own a home
and nice car, I will be _____.

If I have better health, I will _____.

If I eat enough delicious food, have great sex, travel
to enough interesting and exotic places, and
work hard enough, I will finally _____.

If I am at the right place at the right time
in the future, I will _____.

If I discover my soul's purpose, I will _____.

Then ask yourself: Is it true that what
I seek is not already here?

If you let your heart wisdom answer, this last question can be a mind-bender. The strategic mind will be stunned. If you trust your heart's answer and act on it, you will master life's curriculum much more quickly, avoiding some of its remedial dead ends.

As intention clarifies, attention focuses.

Of course, we can gain some degree of transient satisfaction if the above if-then statements are fulfilled, but there will always be an underlying sense of dissatisfaction until the Deep Heart is consciously recognized. Jean Klein often observed that "the object never fulfills its promise."[2] Certainly not for long. Have you noticed that once we attain an object or reach a goal, the hunt is soon on again? Although part of us enjoys the drama of the chase, it is the respite from the search that we most want—the true homecoming.

Once we discover an underlying wholeness in the depths of our being, the relationship to desire changes. We are much less attached to getting what we want and much more grateful for what we have. It is a path of natural contentment rather than willful renunciation. An inner sense of fullness arises that is increasingly independent of circumstances, and we feel happy for no particular reason.

Clarity of Intention and Quality of Attention

How much do you want to know who you really are? Are you willing to give up everything for it? Does your investigation arise from mere intellectual curiosity, or does it come from your heart and guts? As intention clarifies, attention focuses.

The *quality* of your attention is important. If your attention is nonjudgmental, affectionate, and curious, you will be much more intimate with your experience. For example, if you have the story that you *should not* be experiencing what you are actually experiencing, you will remain distant from it.

When we are reacting, it is quite common to think, *Why am I still reacting this way? After all these years of meditation and psychotherapy, why is this still here?* Does this response sound familiar? This way of thinking betrays how conditional our acceptance is. Of course, this is completely normal when we identify with the strategic mind that just wants to feel better and not be bothered with pesky conditioning. However, we *should* on ourselves when we think this way!

One of the powers of the human mind is the ability to envision possibilities. We commonly compare the actual with an ideal, judging *what is* by what we imagine *should be*. We dream up an idealized image and then measure ourselves and others against it. But have you noticed that no one and nothing ever measures up? This way of thinking fosters alienation and estrangement within our self and between our self and others, hindering connection and intimacy, and oppressing spontaneity, creativity, and freedom.

The conditioned mind cannot accept unconditionally.
It always has an agenda, even if it is well-hidden.

The inner judge, posing as a mature adult, is just a child who is a little older than the parts that she or he is judging. We gain our freedom by seeing through the illusion of this critical child's highly limited view. Rational thought is helpful but rarely sufficient. We need to lay our judgments down before the wisdom of the Deep Heart.

Judging obscures the quality of our attention. If we are in judgment of our experience, we can't clearly think, see, listen, or feel. As a result, we can't actually meet our experience as it is. The filter is too thick; the noise is too loud.

If you have traveled on the spiritual path even a little way, you have probably come across some version of "Love what is"—a reminder that you should accept your experience as it is. However, this teaching easily becomes another injunction. Notice the *should* in the earlier sentence—it is always a red flag that the judging mind is at work.

The conditioned mind cannot accept unconditionally. It always has an agenda, even if it is well-hidden. It secretly bargains and sends the message, "I will accept you [sotto voce] if you change or leave." This approach is akin to welcoming guests at your front door while secretly hoping they will exit out the back—the sooner, the better! Guests—our unwanted thoughts, feelings, and sensations—will certainly feel this conditional invitation, even if it is unspoken. As a result, they will be much less willing to enter, relax, and reveal themselves. The result? What we resist, persists. So when your new arrivals show up at your door, put away your timer and share some aromatic green tea and a raspberry scone with them. Settle in and let them tell their stories and share their feelings. They just want to be heard and understood. Once they feel genuinely received, they will be open to a new perspective.

Are you willing to be with your experience just as it is, even if it never changes? This is a critically important checking question. Take a few minutes to inquire with the following practice.

MEDITATIVE INQUIRY
Are You Willing to Accept Your Experience Just as It Is?

Sit quietly where you won't be disturbed, close or lower your eyes, and take a few deep breaths. Feel the weight of your body held by whatever you are sitting on and relax. Feel your attention settling down and in.

Think of a troubling aspect of your conditioning—an unwelcome pattern of behavior, reactive feeling, bodily tension, or invasive thought. Then ask yourself: "Am I willing to accept this just as it is?"

If your response comes from the strategic mind, there will be an honest no. This is good to see. If this is the case, try asking the question a little differently: "Is there something in me that already accepts this just as it is?"

If your attention has settled into the Deep Heart, you will find a yes.

~

Remarkably, the Deep Heart truly and unconditionally loves what is. While discerning, it is free of judgment. It has no timetable for change. It is infinitely patient, kind, and compassionate. Even if you never change, it still loves you unconditionally. This quality of loving awareness is inconceivable to the mind. A mother's love for her child comes closest. Nonetheless, we can tap into and attune with it. Humanity, our own and everyone else's, deeply benefits when we do.

While we can uncover an inherent source of nonjudgmental, compassionate awareness by attuning with the Deep Heart, we can also purposely cultivate beneficent qualities of attention, which is the aim of most mindfulness practices. To some degree, we can learn how to quiet the mind, focus attention, and cultivate lovingkindness (metta), thereby developing relatively open, clear, nonjudgmental, and curious attention. Scientists have recently learned that the brain is surprisingly malleable or "plastic," even in old age. As new networks of neurons are created, the brain rewires itself. These differing paths of uncovering or cultivating essential qualities correspond to the direct and progressive spiritual approaches, which are complementary, each with its benefits and potential pitfalls.

Briefly, the direct path, which is the primary approach of this book, accents the clear and immediate recognition of one's true nature by directly inquiring and sensing into who or what we really are. Essential qualities of being spontaneously radiate out as one's true nature is uncovered, much like a spring that has been unplugged. We are naturally kind, clear, and loving toward others because all beings are known to be essentially the same as ourselves.

The greatest danger of following the direct approach is remaining on an intellectual level. People can fool themselves into thinking that they have fully realized something that they haven't and become stuck in an arrogant mental view as the Deep Heart remains dormant. This seems to happen fairly often, especially among intellectual men who have experienced glimpses of a more profound reality.

On the other hand, the potential downside of the progressive approach is that we become mired in endless seeking and self-improvement, overlooking and postponing an inherent freedom and joy that is always available. Students on a predominantly progressive path will often doubt whether they will ever awaken and recognize their true nature. These types of thoughts impose a subtle yet powerful constraint on the discovery process. For a nuanced discussion of these distinct yet complementary paths, I highly recommend Stephan Bodian's *Beyond Mindfulness*.

Meditation

These days there are increasing numbers of meditation apps available for busy people who are dealing with a wide range of problems from anxiety to poor sleep. These mindfulness-based, problem-focused meditations are helpful on a practical level, but they aren't the kind of meditation that I will be describing. If you are interested in discovering your true nature, a different approach to meditation is needed.

Meditation generally falls into two categories: focused and open (sometimes called concentrative and contemplative). In the focused or concentrative form, the meditator places light attention on a particular object—the breath, an area of the body (such as the center of the chest or lower belly), a mantra, an image, or a positive thought. The purpose of this focused approach is to quiet the mind, to relax the body, or to observe subtle changes in one's experience. In contrast, the open or contemplative style invites us to simply rest in and as open awareness.

At some point we realize that this open, wakeful,
boundless awareness is who we really are.

If you are new to a meditation practice and have difficulty simply resting as open awareness, it can help to begin with a lightly focused approach where you bring your attention to the heart area or the lower belly and imagine breathing in and out from one of these locations. When you become aware that your attention has wandered, as it inevitably will, simply bring it back to your breath and your body. This practice steadies the mind and relaxes the body. It helps if you sit comfortably upright with eyes closed or slightly open, in a place where you won't be disturbed, and at a regular time such as in the morning a few minutes after getting up.

Establishing a ritual time and place is helpful. Be patient. It can take a little while before the mind settles down. Start with ten minutes and then work your way up to twenty or thirty minutes as it feels easier and more natural to sit for longer periods.

Thoughts, feelings, and sensations will continue to come and go, but you will experience a sense of quiet depth, like a swimmer who dives beneath the surface waves. When this starts to happen, simply rest. Give up all subtle effort to focus your attention and simply be as you are. Meditation, at least in the form that I am discussing, is a conscious resting in awareness *as* awareness. Rest as you are, not trying to change anything. Let your thoughts, feelings, and sensations simply be.

There is no one trying to reach a particular state or make something happen. There is just a noticing that all experiences come and go—thoughts (unspoken words, images, plans, and memories) as well as sensations inside and outside the body, some of which we call feelings. Yet we also notice that "something"—we can call it awareness, consciousness, or bare attention—remains throughout it all. As we notice this unchanging background, we open and relax into it. At some point we realize that this open, wakeful, boundless awareness *is* who we really are.

Jean Klein said that when the meditator disappears, there is meditation. I love this statement because it invites us to see that there is no one doing anything, not even meditating. The illusion of an apparently separate observer falls away, as do apparently separate objects of experience. No one is observing, and nothing is being observed. We see that thinking is happening and that no one is thinking; hearing and touching occur without a discrete hearer or toucher. Strange as it may sound, it is quite liberating to realize that we are no one, and it is a huge relief to drop the fiction of being a separate-self.

Adyashanti says that true meditation has no direction or goal.

It is pure wordless surrender, pure silent prayer. All methods aiming at achieving a certain state of mind are limited, impermanent, and conditioned. Fascination with states leads only to bondage and dependency. True meditation is abidance as primordial awareness.

True meditation appears in consciousness spontaneously when awareness is not being manipulated or controlled. When you first start to meditate, you notice that attention is often being held captive by focus on some object: on thoughts, bodily sensations, emotions, memories, sounds, etc. This is because the mind is conditioned to focus and contract upon objects. Then the mind compulsively interprets and tries to control what it is aware of (the object) in a mechanical and distorted way. It begins to draw conclusions and make assumptions according to past conditioning.

In true meditation all objects (thoughts, feelings, emotions, memories, etc.) are left to their natural functioning. This means that no effort should be made to focus on, manipulate, control, or suppress any object of awareness. In true meditation the emphasis is on being awareness; not on being aware of objects, but on resting as primordial awareness itself. Primordial awareness is the source in which all objects arise and subside.

As you gently relax into awareness, into listening, the mind's compulsive contraction around objects will fade. Silence of being will come more clearly into consciousness as a welcoming to rest and abide. An attitude of open receptivity, free of any goal or anticipation, will facilitate the presence of silence and stillness to be revealed as your natural condition.

As you rest into stillness more profoundly, awareness becomes free of the mind's compulsive control, contractions, and identifications. Awareness naturally returns to its non-state of absolute unmanifest potential, the silent abyss beyond all knowing.[3]

It is important to recognize that abiding *in* primordial awareness differs from abiding *as* primordial awareness. If we feel that we are in it, there is still separation—a subtle duality. Our true nature is not a state that we are trying to achieve or rest in. It is who we are, regardless of our experience.

A few days ago, I was sitting in silent meditation, eyes slightly open, with one of my students when I asked him what he was experiencing:

> **Matt**   There is a deep peace. I feel very relaxed and spacious.

> **John**   Is this a state that you are tapping into like a vacation spot you can visit? Or is this who you really are?

> **Matt (after a long silence)**   I never carefully considered this before. You are right. I have been taking this as a peaceful state that I, as a separate-self, access from time to time. In fact, this is who I really am, not separate from anything. Wow!

~ Four ~

MEDITATIVE INQUIRY

*From where does this "I" arise? Seek for it within,
it then vanishes. This is the pursuit of wisdom.*
RAMANA MAHARSHI, *The Teachings of Sri Ramana Marharshi*

MEDITATIVE INQUIRY is the art of sitting with an essential question. It is a complementary practice to silent sitting. You have noticed that I have been inviting you to sit with certain questions. These are forms of meditative inquiry.

Questions arise quite spontaneously from our openness and curiosity. If we want to understand something, we are naturally drawn to investigate it, and we can direct this curiosity to any level of our experience. Einstein pondered several unusual questions in physics and, as a result, developed the special and general theories of relativity, parts of which arose in flashes of sudden insight.

Meditative inquiry can be focused and intentional, even as it remains open-ended. I have developed a version of this potent practice, having refined it over three decades while working with people individually and also while leading self-inquiry groups and retreats for the past fifteen years. I'll outline the basic steps here and then go into each in more detail.

1. Ask yourself if you really want to know.

2. Clarify your question.

3. Allow your attention to settle down and in,
    so that it rests in the heart area.

4. Pose the question and let it go.
    Don't go to the mind for an answer.

5. Be open to a response that can come in any form.

6. Let it in.

7. Act on it.

Ask Yourself If You Really Want to Know

Self-honesty is vital. If you are not really interested in getting to the bottom of something, you won't. If you experience resistance to discovery, be curious about that. Sometimes we feel ambivalent about finding out what's really true—we may not want to know what we know. Important discoveries may require us to change our lives in a significant way, so if you are fearful, lean into it. Reality is almost always kinder than your thoughts.

We need to allow attention to settle into the heart area
if we are going to access a different kind of knowing.

I was recently speaking with a European woman during an online event who wondered if she had the courage to let go into the Deep Heart.

"If I open to the Great Heart, I am afraid that it will tear me to pieces!" she said, trembling with fear and aliveness.

As I listened, she could see that I did not share her fear.

"It's not true, is it? It's just my mind, isn't it?" she asked.

"Yes," I replied. "The mind projects its worst fears onto the unknown. Let yourself shake; you'll be okay."

Her trembling initially increased, and her eyes widened in fear. After another minute, she began to relax, and a beautiful smile broke across her face like the sunrise. Her eyes welled up with gratitude, and she laughed with delight.

"Trusting this Universal Heart is the only thing that really matters. I feel myself at home now. It is as if there is only one great beating heart that is not separate from anything or anyone."

"Yes," I added, "It is seamless, undivided. You are home."

Clarify Your Question

Ask your question as clearly as you can. What is the gist of it? What do you really want to know? Distill it down to as few words as possible and check with your body to sense if you have done so. There will be a sense of rightness when you have.

Sometimes it can take time to home in on your true question. Other times it will be immediately obvious. Clarifying your question leads you to an answer, which is why spiritual teachers will often ask their students to sit with their questions first before posing them since questions will often resolve on their own. You are beginning to enter into a dialogue with the inner teacher—your own knowing.

Allow Attention to Settle Down and In, so That It Rests in the Heart Area

We usually don't do this when we want an answer. Instead, we try to think about our problem or question. However, it is our thinking that usually is the problem! We need to allow attention to settle into the heart area if we are going to access a different kind of knowing.

It can be helpful to close your eyes, take a few deep breaths, and relax. Feel your feet touching the floor (if you are seated) and let the weight of your body be held by whatever you are sitting upon. Remind yourself that you don't know, can't know, and don't need to know an answer with your ordinary mind. The willingness to not know creates space for a different kind of knowing, for heart wisdom to emerge.

Allow your forehead and eyes to relax, and let your attention settle down and in. Imagine that you can directly inhale from and exhale into the space in front of your heart area. Place your hand on the center of your chest if this helps. Allow your attention to rest here innocently, as you sense your breath and your chest.

Pose the Question and Let It Go; Don't Go to the Mind for an Answer

The central question of self-inquiry is "Who or what am I?" Pose it mentally to your heart area and then let it go, like dropping a stone into a still pool. Toss it in, be quiet, and listen and feel what happens.

You might feel a strong temptation to start thinking about your question, especially if you are new to this approach. Avoid this if you can. Your thinking mind has chewed on your question enough. If you go to your mind for an answer, your attention will once more take the elevator back to your forehead—an extremely familiar and limited upper floor. I can always tell when someone is in their mind trying to answer an essential question because their hands flutter around their heads as they speak (furthermore, they typically say things like "I think" or "I believe" a lot).

Be Open to a Response That Can Come in Any Form

When our body is relatively relaxed and open, we can tap into a holistic sense of the truth. This is called a *felt sense*—a term coined by Eugene Gendlin, who developed an inner search process in the 1960s called *focusing*.[1] A felt sense is a preverbal, whole-body sense of something vague that arises before our sensations, feelings, and thoughts separate. Everyone has a native capacity for felt sensing, although most people are not consciously aware of it. It can be learned with a little time and attention.

When we open ourselves to heart wisdom, we open our conditioned body-mind to the light of awareness.

When we drop a question into the heart area and don't go to the ordinary mind for an answer, we are opening to this felt sense. The response may first come as a subtle sensation—a vibration, for example—or it may come as a faint feeling or sensation somewhere in the body.

If we are wired visually, our response may arise as an image that may or may not also be accompanied by sensations, feelings, or words. Ordinarily distinct modes of sensing and thinking tend to blend. Our best poets and writers have access to this multidimensional level, weaving their magic with surprising words and images.

Sometimes a wordless knowing arises—a vibrant silence. For instance, when we explore the truth of our core limiting beliefs, we often come in touch with a wordless knowing of their irrelevance. If we inquire into who we really are, we will quickly come to a "don't know." This is not a mistake. It signals that we have gone as far as the ordinary mind can go. We have made a critically important discovery—the limit of the mind's ability to know that which is not an object. The mind is designed to grasp ideas just as our hands are designed to grasp objects, but the mind is incapable of grasping the infinite. This realization brings a letting go and a new kind of openness—an openness to being open.

Let It In

When we open ourselves to heart wisdom, we open our conditioned body-mind to the light of awareness. When this happens, it often feels as if separate and frozen compartments within our body are being touched by warmth and light. As we open to a deeper truth, we can often feel an interior softening and melting—the inner armor is softening; the inner ice is melting.

The individual body-mind—what we ordinarily take to be our self—has been under the effect of powerful conditioning for many years. This conditioning leaves its imprint on the way that we consciously and subconsciously think, feel, sense, and act. We have been innocently dividing, freezing, numbing, armoring, coiling, ignoring, and attacking ourselves from an early age, and this divisive and self-protective process has tremendous momentum. It takes time for it to undo itself. The stronger the conditioning, both in terms of intensity and duration, the longer this unwinding process takes. While this conditioning can substantially diminish, I doubt if it ever ends.

We can also think of this conditioning process as misprogramming. If you put faulty information into a computerized system, the system will malfunction. Our body-mind responds in a similar way. When we are young, we are highly prone to being misprogrammed since we are unable to maturely understand what we are experiencing—for example, if we are treated badly, we believe that we are bad. Parents inevitably hand down their own undigested subconscious patterns inherited from prior generations. It is an ancient process of transmitting ignorance, confusion, and suffering.

As the light of awareness begins to saturate the conditioned body-mind, we unlearn what we thought and felt was true. As we decondition and deprogram, we simultaneously attune and orient to our true nature. Our vibrational level upgrades. We can support this process by consciously cooperating with it—letting in our insights, feeling the shifts and openings in our body, and breathing it all in so even our cells participate in the process.

If we don't let in our new insights and felt senses of truth, they can be easily relegated to memory. You probably wouldn't discard nuggets of gold so you could check your email or browse the web, so take your time to let in these gems of light when they arise. Slow down and let in the radiance of your true nature. Savor it without grasping.

Act on It

It is one thing to let the light of awareness saturate your body-mind; it's another entirely to let it move you in your daily life. Acting on your heart wisdom creates a virtuous cycle, reinforcing your questioning, listening, and discovery, which in turn fosters self-trust, self-confidence, and inner sovereignty. Self-trust is actually a trust in the current of loving awareness that underlies all of life.

How Does Your Deepest Knowing
Want to Act Through You?

If there is something obvious to do, do it! If you are feeling cautious about implementing your inner knowing, test it out with small gestures and notice the results. I have repeatedly trusted my inner knowing with all of the major decisions in my life, whether entering into relationships, pursuing a career, or following a spiritual path. I am so grateful that I have.

~

Partnered, or Dyadic, Meditative Inquiry

You can practice meditative inquiry by yourself or with a partner in a dyad, or twosome. Practicing with a partner introduces a powerful relational dimension. By having someone pose a question to you, you no longer need to ask it yourself, which frees you to completely be with the process of inner listening. Additionally, when you verbalize your responses to someone else, it brings your inner knowing more clearly into conscious awareness, and this helps clarify your search for words and images that are congruent with an unfolding inner response. Finally, you navigate being with another person as you tap into your heart wisdom. This is one the most rewarding parts of the dyadic process as you share the discoveries of the Deep Heart and open yourself to experiencing an essential communion with another person.

I always include a period of dyadic meditative inquiry during my retreats, even if they are only day-long events. It has become an essential component that beautifully complements listening to talks, dialoguing, body sensing, and quietly meditating. When people share their discoveries during the closing circle of a retreat, they often report that their experiences during the dyadic inquiry were the most revelatory and impactful.

Here's a brief summary of the process.

Pick a time and place where you won't be interrupted. Decide on a question you want to explore and who will pose the question first.[2] Sit across from one another, close your eyes, relax, and settle in. Take a minute to first sense and breathe into your lower belly, heart area, and forehead (between and slightly above the eyebrows) respectively. Then take a minute to attune with each other on the level of being, first with eyes closed and then with eyes open in a soft gaze. When you feel attuned with your partner (without leaving your sense of being grounded and centered within yourself), begin.

One partner poses the question at a pace set by the listener, who signals when she or he is ready to be asked. As the listener, don't go to your mind for an answer. Be willing to be surprised. Be sure to leave time for silence. Feel free to open or close your eyes and to share whatever arises or remain silent. As the questioner, simply listen as if you are listening to yourself (which you are) and wait to be cued by the listener before posing the question again. Otherwise, don't respond verbally. It is important that the pace feels natural and unhurried. Reverse roles after ten minutes or so; then debrief.

~

Meditative Gazing

Meditative gazing is an elegant, powerful, and liberating practice in itself. It is a fast track to profound intimacy that astonishes people who are new to it. I find that it can be a useful complement to solitary meditative practices, evoking both personal and transpersonal dimensions that otherwise remain dormant. People imagine that this kind of gazing is suitable only for intimate partners, but this isn't the case and, sadly, far too many partners and friends never experience the degree of closeness offered by this practice. Since feelings of closeness are often associated with sexual intimacy, it is important to differentiate these phenomena and to clarify boundaries beforehand.

When people feel safe, relaxed, and open enough to settle in together with one another, gazing can evoke and reinforce the sense of shared being. We all have a strong desire to be seen just as we are—unadorned with any story of who we think we are—and being seen this way can result in a profoundly revelatory release from the inner prison of the separate-self. I repeatedly find that there's a sense of relief and gratitude when we transparently share presence.

Being on the receiving end of a steady, warm, loving, and attuned gaze is intrinsically healing.

Yet we are also afraid to be seen. This is especially true when we believe that we are fundamentally lacking or flawed. If we believe that we will be unmasked as the deficient and damaged person we secretly think and feel that we are, we will naturally resist being seen. Shame and fear are interwoven aspects of our body-mind conditioning. We resist feeling these two compelling and difficult emotions—ashamed of our fear and afraid of our shame. We can spend years hiding what we don't want to be seen from ourselves and others, all the while feeling like a fraud.

However, when we open ourselves to the warm, open, and accepting gaze of another trusted person, our unloved and unwelcomed parts inevitably come to the surface. It's hard to maintain our mask—the idealized image of how we want to be seen—with this practice. We may initially feel anxious and experience sensations of contraction in the interior of the body, and we may think and feel that our partner can see everything that is wrong with us and fear that they will reject and abandon us. In this way, we can unconsciously project our self-critic onto our partner. While we ordinarily do this to a minor degree with everyone we meet, it comes up dramatically during gazing practice.

Our pace of moving through this zone of the psyche depends upon our level of self-acceptance and self-love. Whether we pass through it quickly or slowly, a powerful process of transformation unfolds. Those parts that have been hidden and unwelcomed feel felt, seen, and warmly embraced, which all fosters self-acceptance. Since most psychological wounding is relational in origin, being on the receiving end of a steady, warm, loving, and attuned gaze is intrinsically healing. It is also healing to be able to offer this to another person and to witness its impact.

BODY SENSING PRACTICE 1

The Practice of Gazing

Follow the same initial instructions as with meditative inquiry, but rather than posing a question, simply remain in a relaxed, noneffortful, and nonintentional meditative gaze with one another for as long as it feels natural. Feel free to speak from time to time, describing your experience or remaining in silence. Your eyes may naturally open and close as you practice awareness together. Simply be open to whatever unfolds and debrief at the end.

~

Mirror Gazing

If you don't have a gazing partner at the moment, you can find one in a mirror! In this solo variation of the practice there is little doubt that you are looking at yourself. Approach it in the same way as you would while gazing with another person: sustain a relaxed gaze with the reflection of your eyes, don't focus on your physical appearance or any judgments you have about that, and let yourself fall into your own depths. Rest as the primordial awareness that you are.

~ Five ~

THE BODY AS VIBRATION AND SPACE

Breath flows in and then surrenders to flow out again.
In this moment, drink eternity.
Breath flows out, emptying, emptying.
Offering itself to infinity.
Cherishing these moments,
Mind dissolves into heart,
Heart dissolves into space,
Body becomes a shimmering field
Pulsating between emptiness and fullness.

LORIN ROCHE, *The Radiance Sutras*

FOR MILLENNIA, INDIAN, Tibetan, and Chinese yogis have described increasingly subtle layers and flows of an energy body that coexists within and around the physical body. One version entails seven major energy centers (chakras) aligned along a central vertical channel (sushumna) with both ascending and descending flows of energy. For those who are kinesthetically sensitive, these phenomena are quite palpable. For a detailed discussion of the psycho-spiritual significance of these major energy centers, please see chapter 2 of my book *In Touch*.

Descriptions of a multidimensional energy body complement descriptions of the body that focus more on anatomy and physiology.

We don't need to take these portrayals at face value or dismiss them as pure fancy; instead, they can serve as tentative pointers for our own in-depth explorations. Now that scientists have discovered that the human eye can detect a single photon, it's likely that we will in time be able to objectively verify that we can track internal body signals, interoceiving subtle dimensions of our felt experience.[1] For now, subjective accounts of subtle sensing will necessarily vary depending on individual practitioners and their cultures.

Be open to the possibility that your body is not what you think it is.

This model of a multidimensional body applies directly to the theme of the Deep Heart. I would not write about the importance of the heart unless I knew it intimately firsthand and also understood its critical role in psychological healing and spiritual awakening. If there are, as I propose, layers to the heart ranging from the relatively gross, through the refined, to the transcendent, then many of us will be able to directly or indirectly sense this in some way.

One of the easiest ways to sense the emotional and energetic reality of the heart area is to notice what we sense and feel when we fall in love or, conversely, when we lose someone we have loved via death or a painful breakup. Heart openings are intoxicatingly joyful, and heart breaks are extraordinarily painful. Have you ever wondered why this is the case? Are the opening and closing of the heart purely physiological, or might something else be going on? We will explore romantic love in a later chapter, but for now I'll just acknowledge the central role that the heart area plays in human relationships and in genuine spiritual openings. The majority of popular songs and a large number of our most compelling stories revolve around love found and lost.

In order to explore your heart in any depth, it's helpful to sense your whole body with as few ideas as possible. Clear the slate—be open to the possibility that your body is *not* what you think it is. Rather than approaching your body as a familiar solid object made up of skin, bones, muscles, organs, tissues, and cells governed by neural and hormonal networks, I encourage you to approach it differently—as a field of vibration filled with space.

In the next two exercises, you will first experience the body as a field of vibration and then, in turn, as pure space. These meditations are inspired by the *Vijnanabhairava Tantra*, a key experiential text in Kashmiri Tantric Shaivism that was authored over a thousand years ago.[2] As I suggested in the introduction, it's a good idea to record these guided meditations on your smartphone, and I recommend pausing between the steps outlined below for at least twenty seconds. Including the pauses, please allow for at least ten minutes in total. Find a quiet place where you won't be disturbed, sit comfortably, and close your eyes.

BODY SENSING PRACTICE 2
Sensing the Body as Vibration

Take a few deep breaths and allow your attention to settle down and in.

Feel the weight of your body being held by whatever you are sitting on and let yourself be completely held.

Sense the bottoms of your feet, the tips of your toes, and notice a lively vibration. Imagine it growing stronger, gradually enveloping both feet, and then moving up both legs.

Sense the palms of your hands and the tips of your fingers. Notice a subtle vibration—a sense of aliveness. Feel it enveloping both hands and slowly spreading up both arms.

Feel this sense of vibrant aliveness growing into your hips and shoulders.

And then into the belly and the chest, including your back.

Sense this lively vibration moving up the neck and into the head, suffusing the mouth, ears, eyes, and brain. Take your time.

Now let go of any focusing and sense your entire body as a diffuse field of lively vibration. Notice that it is difficult to tell exactly where your body ends and where the so-called world begins. Allow this sense of vibration to extend out into space in all directions: front . . . back . . . left . . . right . . . up . . . and down.

Rest in and as this expansive sense of vibrant spaciousness as long as you like.

~

Many people are astonished to discover that their body is vibrant and expansive rather than static and dense. Further, they are delighted to sense that they are not bound to a separate-inside-self. Jean Klein likened the body to a musical instrument.[3] Our bodies are indeed capable of experiencing and expressing amazing beauty when they are well-tuned, and we tune and awaken the body by sensing its vibratory nature. Rather than feeling numb, tense, and dense as a result of neglect and abuse, our body starts to awaken and reveal subtle textures and tones that are directly related to what we're experiencing in the moment, as well as by what has been stored in our psychosomatic memory. As the interior of the body opens up and flowers, a secret garden unfolds. Jean Klein would sometimes call this the "Edenic" body, alluding to the mythic garden that we left long ago.[4] Eden is never far away.

While some people are naturally more attuned to their body, all of us can learn to listen more carefully. We just need to pay attention and inquire in an open way with such questions as "What is it that I am sensing?" and "What am I actually experiencing right now?" Take a few deep breaths, slow down, be quiet, and sense into the interior of your body for a few minutes. Don't approach your body as if you are a distant observer. Enter into it. Breathe into it. Sense into it. Feel it from the inside. Inhabit it.

When we can sense the continuous space within and around our body, we no longer feel so trapped.

As we begin to sense into our body, some areas will feel more free and open while others will feel dense and closed. It is common to encounter areas that feel numb or frozen, and this is often true with the heart area. As I mentioned in chapter 1, when we are young, we learn to protect our most sensitive areas from attack, abandonment, neglect, and the shocks of ordinary life. When it's too painful to stay open, we find ways to shut down. We withdraw our native sensitivity like a turtle pulling back into its shell. We try to be as small, invisible, or hard as possible in order to remain safe and avoid difficult feelings such as shame, terror, grief, rage, vulnerability, or bitter disappointment. Sometimes, under extreme duress, we may even need to dissociate and leave our body for a while.

This tendency to contract becomes habitual. We gradually armor ourselves on the physical level with chronic muscular tension, on the emotional level by suppressing or completely denying our feelings, and on the energetic level by numbing and walling off. We freeze and harden and then subconsciously identify with this condition. We feel and think that this is really who we are. It's as if we take the icy walls and bars of a self-constructed prison as our self.

Discovering a felt sense of space is powerful medicine for this delusional identification. When we can sense the continuous space within and around our body, we no longer feel so trapped. We are tapping into an inherent sense of spaciousness that is our birthright. Importantly, we are not creating space—instead, we are acknowledging the spacious awareness that is already here.

The setup for the following practice is the same as the former one in terms of finding a time and place where you won't be interrupted and prerecording the steps on your smartphone. Again, be sure to allow ample time for the pauses.

BODY SENSING PRACTICE 3
Sensing the Body as Space

Take a few deep breaths and allow your attention to settle down and in.

Feel the weight of your body being held by whatever you are sitting on and let yourself be completely held.

Feel into the interior of your body, slowly scanning the sensations from the tips of your toes to the top of your head. Imagine that you can directly breathe into and out from each area of your body that you are sensing. Take a few minutes with this step. If your attention drifts, just return to the last area that you were feeling and continue.

Notice a sense of space within your whole body, as if it were a grand cathedral or temple filled with space. Because we know from physics that even the tiniest sub-particles are filled with space, it must be true for your physical body as well.

Begin to sense the space around your body, first in front and then behind. Feel yourself breathing in from and out to this space. Each breath expands the space feeling.

Do the same, first to the left side and then to the right side, continuing to breathe in from and out into each side. Let the exhalation completely empty itself before beginning the inhalation.

Now sense and breathe into the overhead space, feeling into the heavens. After a little while, do the same with the space beneath your body, feeling into the depths of the ground, allowing your exhalation to completely empty.

Sense the space globally in all directions simultaneously.

Bring your attention to the boundary between the space inside your body and the space outside. Is the space any different? Is there really a boundary at all?

Feel the space within your body and around your body as one space. Be this space. Rest as this space for as long as you like.

~

With both of the body sensing practices, carefully notice the transition from a meditative to a more ordinary state before you get up. As you observe this shift, you support the integrative process of feeling more vibrant and spacious in your daily life. I suggest that you devote yourself to a two-week experiment with each of these practices in order to fairly assess their impact. There is little value in simply reading about them.

My wife, Christiane, studied with Jean Klein for over twenty years and now shares his "body approach"—a special style of yoga based on the Kashmiri tradition I mentioned earlier. Practitioners sense the body moment to moment as it slowly moves through a series of gentle poses without trying to achieve anything, welcoming every experience that arises (including resistance) while accenting the feeling of vast space. As Christiane elegantly shares this approach during our retreats, people often report experiencing their body in an entirely new way. It is a radically different practice from the goal-oriented, athletic, and secular yoga that is so commonly taught these days.

Learning to sense the spacious and vibrant nature of the body makes us more available to recognize our true nature as infinite loving awareness. It also offers an extremely valuable resource to deal with our more challenging experiences.

~ Six ~

STEPPING BACK FROM, INTO, AND THROUGH EXPERIENCE

In the openness of our true nature,
we are free to be a human form . . .
free to be real instead of needing to be perfect.
DOROTHY HUNT, *Ending the Search*

THERE ARE TWO complementary ways to be with our inner experiences whether they take the form of thoughts, feelings, sensations, or some combination of these. The first way is to step back completely, taking refuge in and as pure awareness. The other approach is to step right into and through the center of an experience where it is sensed in the body. Stepping back from an experience is a movement of disidentification and corresponds with a transcendent approach to life. Stepping into experience and fully embracing it corresponds with an immanent and Tantric approach.[1]

Stepping Back

Being able to step away from the *content* of our experience into its *context*—in other words, the infinite space of loving awareness—encourages feelings of spaciousness, freedom, clarity, and peace. No matter what we are experiencing, we are always aware of it. Everything is happening in us as open awareness.

For example, whenever you have a thought, you must first be aware of it. This simple but critically important differentiation is reflected in our ordinary speech. We say: "*I am* aware of thought" or "*I am* thinking about . . ." Prior to any thought is the "I am"—the sense of being aware. Awareness precedes thought, even if we don't consciously recognize it. We can be aware without thought when there are moments of conscious silence, yet we can never have a thought without being implicitly aware. Our attention can certainly be lost or absorbed in thought, yet a quiet background awareness is always present, available with a slight shift of attention.

At any moment we can disembark from a train of thought and consciously abide as open, content-less awareness. Just as all sounds arise from and resolve in silence, all thoughts arise from and dissolve in awareness. Recognizing this is tremendously freeing. We can simply and knowingly *be* at any moment.

Our essential freedom is always available.

This principle applies equally to feelings and sensations. What we call our inner or outer world is a synthesis of various complex sensations, colored by memory. However, without awareness, there is no "world." Every apparent object that we perceive is shaped and filtered by our consciousness and interpretation. What we experience as our world is simply a construct.

The differentiation of awareness from experience is often illustrated by metaphors—pixilated images on LCD, a movie on a cinema screen, words on a page, or reflections in a mirror. Even before there were televisions, movies, books, or mirrors, there were images reflected on water and shadows cast upon rock walls—consider Plato's allegory of the cave. These related analogies, used by spiritual teachers and philosophers for thousands of years, point to the fact that our attention is easily absorbed by our thoughts, feelings, and sensations—so much so that we believe in and identify with them, overlooking a simple, primordial, background awareness that precedes them.

Discovering an implicit background awareness is profoundly liberating. It's like prisoners who turn around in amazement to finally discover that there is no rear wall to their cells. Regardless of our experience, we can always fall back into and as awareness, taking refuge as infinite space. Our essential freedom is always available.

When we are able to step or fall back from our experience, we are able to witness it from a more expansive perspective. We notice that thoughts, feelings, and sensations come and go while awareness remains. This awareness allows us to loosen our grip of identity on these experiences. If these hectoring thoughts, disturbing emotions, and uncomfortable sensations are always changing, what is it that never comes or goes? Could this be what I really am?

This is why the first step toward recognizing our true nature is almost always a negation of who we ordinarily think and feel we are. This is the *via negativa*, or negative way. The Greek term *kenosis* means an emptying out—in this case, an emptying out of illusions (a disillusionment in the best sense). This approach emphasizes that we are *not* the contents of our consciousness; in fact, we are not any "thing" at all. We are no one, no thing. Our true nature cannot be objectified.

We are ultimately undefinable and thus totally *free from* everything. This is one of the premier insights of traditional nondual teachings. "You mean I am not bound by my thoughts and their related feelings in any way? Who I really am is pure awareness or consciousness?" We are invited by these teachings to wake *up* out of our mis-taken identity and simply be as we are, undefined and unconfined by any story or image. Can you sense the liberating power of this realization?

When this initial revelation actually lands, part of our egocentric conditioning spontaneously falls away. We experience tremendous inner relief when we recognize our inherent freedom and finally witness conditioning from spacious awareness. However, significant levels of our conditioning remain untouched by this initial mental awakening. Many people who have experienced some degree of awakening from the mind—in which they feel significantly freed from their conscious thoughts and images—are puzzled and disappointed by this phenomenon. They find themselves still caught in and acting out painful and dysfunctional patterns of conditioning, even as they witness them.

Has something gone wrong? Not at all. It just means that the process of awakening needs to saturate less conscious emotional, instinctive, and somatic levels of conditioning. Waking up is not enough. We also need to wake down and in—all the way through the body.

Simply put, we cannot engage in life
if we are disengaged from our experience.

I recall attending a meeting of spiritual friends some years ago. One member of our group—an older male steeped in traditional nondual teachings—strongly asserted that if someone experiences difficult emotions, they should not focus on them but instead turn their attention upward to the vastness of the sky—in other words, be the witness to their experience. I found this to be a familiar, transcendent prescription, one that unfortunately tends to foster avoidance rather than genuine transcendence, the results of which were evident in his own life. It is true that we can temporarily step back from our challenging conditioning for respite and perspective, but our conditioning will always return until we meet it more intimately. Unwelcomed guests will keep knocking at the door until we receive them fully.

It can be difficult to be vulnerable and willing to face each experience as it is. It takes humility, courage, and understanding to do so. We can easily use a spiritual philosophy or a state of temporary inner peace to avoid this encounter.

The bulk of our conditioning is subconscious. Most of our emotional and somatic reactions can be traced to our subconscious thinking, but some of our reactions precede any thought at all because they happen prior to the brain's ability to formulate thought. All of these reactions, whether sub- or preconscious, are embedded in the body and the nervous system, originating from some form of poor bonding with our primary caretakers, from trauma, or from both. The transcendent approach that emphasizes disidentification is rarely sufficient to significantly touch and transform the level of conditioning that comes with developmental trauma.

Stepping Into and Through

If we are interested in being intimate with life—in being *free* to be here—we need to be willing to fully step into our experience just as it is. Simply put, we cannot engage in life if we are disengaged from our experience. This means that we are willing to uncover and question the truth of our limiting subconscious beliefs, fully feel our feelings, and completely sense our sensations.

So, when is it necessary to so carefully attend to our experience? Isn't conditioning endless? *Yes.* Isn't there a danger of getting side-tracked into some kind of self-improvement project, postponing the recognition of our implicit freedom? *Yes.* Isn't it easy for the ego to re-engage by using psycho-spiritual methods and having an agenda for healing and integration? *Yes.* These are all legitimate questions and potential problems.

Clearly, the path of immanence also has its pitfalls. Just as the path of transcendence can be co-opted by the separate sense of self in order to avoid or dissociate from life, the path of immanence can be co-opted by the ego to prolong the apparent seeker and the endless search for purification. It is important to be aware of these subtle egocentric strategies; both paths have their legitimate roles to play, and each has its potential limitations.

This is why scrupulous, heartfelt self-honesty is so important—the willingness to stay open to the revelation and unfolding of our most fundamental truth. After Adya's initial awakening, he heard an inner voice say, "Keep going."[2] This voice was an expression of the same current of inner wisdom and love in each of us that guides this process to more fully recognize who we are and what life is. It is impersonal yet extraordinarily intimate, emanating from the core of our being.

In the same way that it guides us toward waking up, it also steers us toward waking down and in. It advises us at times to step back from life's expressions into our essential nature as timeless, spacious, wakeful, loving awareness, and other times to fully step into life's play. Adya describes this cyclical movement as "love returning for itself"—a concise and poignant formulation.[3] Our true nature wants to be fully embodied, and the true nature of the body as loving awareness wants to be fully revealed.

The question of when and how to be with our conditioning needs to be governed by something other than our strategic mind. If there is a "should" in our approach, we are off the mark. The more we are able to be quiet and tune in to our heart wisdom, the clearer our guidance will be. For example, I was recently working with one of my students as he explored a subtle abandonment reaction that was creating discord in his primary relationship. He could sense a small, dense contraction localized at the base of his spine related to the fear of annihilation. After sitting quietly for another minute, he could also sense that it was being spontaneously bathed in a field of gold light.

"I know that I could try to breathe this light into the contraction in order to speed up the process, but this feels too willful and unnecessary," he said.

"Yes," I agreed, "It is enough to let them both be there together at the same time, isn't it?"

He was following his inner guidance. No further effort was needed. A crucial aspect of his conditioning relating to an early complex bond with his mother was softening, opening, and updating, and a current of heart wisdom moved through both of us, supporting this integrative and healing process.

I used to follow an informal "three knocks" rule in terms of knowing when to attend to an aspect of my own conditioning: if a pattern recurred, I'd pay attention to it and delve in; if not, I'd simply observe it arising and passing away. It's not a bad rule of thumb, but I think a more intuitive and precise approach is to get quiet and tap into our heart wisdom: "What is my deepest knowing about this reaction? Do I need to attend to this? If so, in what way?" We listen and follow, rather than trying to avoid or grasp.

All of our experience arises and falls within our awareness, which is the ground of who we are.

Reality is both unmoving and moving, profoundly still and exuberantly dynamic. Tantric Shaivism has a wonderful word for this:

spanda—meaning "sacred pulse" or "oscillation." The nondual teachings of traditional Advaita Vedanta describe the ultimate nature of reality as being essentially silent and still, in other words—static. By extension, the phenomenal world is described as an appearance or an illusion (maya) that lacks any essential reality. In contrast, the Tantric view sees both the unchanging and changing sides of life as being real and embraces life's dynamic expressions, rather than subtly devaluing them. Instead of simply dismissing our bodies as *not* who we are, the Tantric approach treasures our bodies as essential expressions of reality. In my opinion, Tantra offers a more balanced approach than traditional Advaita, embracing both the formless and formed dimensions of our experience as well as masculine and feminine dispositions. Interestingly, contemporary forms of Advaita are increasingly incorporating Tantric elements.

Here's an outline of the basic steps of my approach to facing and exploring our conditioning, each of which I examine in depth below.

1. Start from spacious presence as much as possible.

2. Be willing to be intimate with your experience rather than trying to change or get rid of it.

3. Enter through the body, not the mind.

4. Allow time to both feel your feelings and sense your sensations.

5. Inquire: "What is in the core of this feeling or sensation?"

6. If needed, also ask, "Is there a core limiting belief that goes with this?" and then, "What is my deepest knowing about this belief?"

7. Let in the shift and the understanding.

START FROM SPACIOUS PRESENCE AS MUCH AS POSSIBLE

Spacious presence is our fundamental nature and greatest resource. It is the greatest re-source because it the *source* of all experience. As we have seen, all of our experience arises and falls within our awareness, which is the ground of who we are. The more we can approach our experience from our essential nature as open, wakeful, loving, spacious awareness or presence, the more intimate and liberating our contact will be. Presence offers the optimal field for experience to unfold. Here are a few pointers to help you tap into spacious presence:

- Sit quietly, take a few deep breaths, notice your present experience, and then notice that you are aware of your experience.

- Shift your attention to this awareness and to the feeling of an expansive, intimate field. Rest in and as this awareness knowingly.

- Sense your body as a vibrant form in open spaciousness.

- Feel into the warmth and openness of the heart area.

BE WILLING TO BE INTIMATE WITH YOUR EXPERIENCE RATHER THAN TRYING TO CHANGE OR GET RID OF IT

The more you want to change or get rid of your experience, the stronger the resistance you'll encounter. Check your agenda at the door. Just be open to what is here in the moment, innocently exploring. The point is to become intimate with what is here, not to change it. Trust that when there is a real meeting, transformation will naturally unfold, and for now it is enough to be open to understanding and feeling something new—the rest will take care of itself. The more that we accept ourselves as we are, the more open we are to natural change.

ENTER THROUGH THE BODY, NOT THE MIND

I have found that it is generally more useful to approach our experience through feelings and sensations, rather than our thoughts. If beliefs are an important element, which they often are, we will get to them more directly by first grounding attention in our body. Initially focusing on sensations tends to short-circuit the problem-solving, interpretive thinking mode, and this allows for a more natural "making sense of experience" to happen both during and after an inner exploration.

A feeling is a special kind of sensation. Where is it felt most acutely in your body? If there are multiple areas, pick one to focus on and breathe into it. What is its texture? Does it have a shape? Be curious, open, and affectionate. Let go of any judgment that you should not be feeling what you are feeling. Doing so only creates distance.

If you don't feel anything and remember little of your childhood, it is almost always because it was too emotionally painful to do so at the time. Feelings may have been suppressed or devalued in your upbringing even if you felt relatively stable and safe. Emotional literacy may not have been part of your ethnic culture or family of origin—for example, expressions of overt anger were strongly suppressed in my family, and I didn't clearly know when I was angry until I left home for college. The good news is that we can always learn.

If you are out of touch with your feelings, pay attention to sensations in your body, especially those in the interior of your chest and belly. If you don't recognize what you are feeling, breathe and sense into your experience until you do—for instance, a diffuse sense of agitation may clarify as a feeling of fear or anger. Numbness may open into emotional hurt. If you are generally not aware of your feelings, try labeling them, but once you recognize a particular feeling, be sure to let go of the label and just feel it as sensation.

Conversely, sometimes a wave of emotion can be so strong that we are overwhelmed by it in the moment. An emotional storm may need to pass before we are calm and clear enough to more intimately approach it. In such cases, it is more useful to resource ourselves first. This may mean focusing on an area of our body that feels peaceful and relaxed or turning our attention to the outer environment and doing something calming and grounding. We can learn to move our attention back and forth (pendulation) from a hyperaroused inner state to a calm one, as well as take our difficult experiences in smaller doses (titration).[4]

If an emotional state is too intense to bear, you can also experiment with placing your attention on its polarity or opposite. Once it is in the foreground of your attention, let both emotional polarities coexist in your awareness. For example, sit with shame and innocence, or rage and the feeling of empowerment, and notice what happens.[5]

A beneficent letting go is happening.
You are going sane.

Discover those genuine resources that truly nourish and support you and use them as needed—self-inquiry, meditation, yoga, Chi Gung, bodywork, journaling, reading, a walk in nature, a warm bath, a nap, or chatting with a good friend. Sense into what your system needs. You can also evoke and tap in memories of needed inner resources, such as peace or safety.[6]

Additionally, it can often be helpful to rely on professional help to navigate chronically hyperaroused nervous systems. The clear, grounded, and well-attuned relational attention of another person may be an essential ingredient in your healing, and some of us need the support and attuned input of another human being in order to better self-regulate.

ALLOW TIME TO BOTH FEEL YOUR FEELINGS AND SENSE YOUR SENSATIONS

Our experience is constantly changing—always in subtle ways and sometimes dramatically. Take a few minutes to just feel and sense what is here now. As you learn to pay attention in new ways, you will probably notice slight shifts in your feelings and sensations. They may dissolve on their own as you receive them in the simple light of presence. Deeper levels may begin to unveil themselves, or areas of numbness may start coming to life. You might occasionally tremble, shake, or cry. Let your experience unfold. A beneficent letting go is happening. You are going sane.

INQUIRE: "WHAT IS IN THE CORE OF THIS FEELING OR SENSATION?"

It's useful to introduce this question after we've allowed our feelings and sensations to be as they are for a few minutes. We innocently pose the question and let go, not going to our thinking mind for an answer. This step usually leads to increased intimacy with our experience as subconscious and unconscious layers bubble up with surprising responses. It's not unusual for the treasure hidden within a shadowy feeling to reveal itself. For instance, if we ask what's in the core of our feeling-sensation of unworthiness, we may discover a radiant sense of being. In this way, we encounter aspects of our native wholeness.

Sometimes we will see a core pattern and its origin. For example, we may see that we have been carrying a pattern of conditioning from one of our parents who inherited it from their parents before them. These patterns are often passed down across multiple generations, which is not surprising given the collective hardships that humanity has endured. Contacting the cross-generational nature of our conditioning will often lead to more understanding, compassion, and a spontaneous letting go: "This doesn't belong to me, and I no longer need to carry it for them." We start to see that none of our familial conditioning is personal. It never belonged to anyone, really. Essentially, all we've done is inherited misunderstanding.

Sometimes an underlying beneficent energy gets misdirected. Rage, for instance, has a healthy life-protective energy buried within it, but because this life-affirming impulse was not allowed healthy expression early on, we may have felt powerless and subsequently began to desperately lash out at everyone. Empowerment is the medicine for rage.

Rather than surfacing essential insights, qualities, or energies, sometimes our inquiry takes us directly back to spacious awareness where we realize in a flash of astonishment that *this awareness* is the source and substance of everything, including our conditioning. It is quite a revelation to discover infinite space in the center of our tightest contractions. This discovery starts to make sense once we see that somatic contractions were attempts to protect what was most sensitive and precious within us.

ASK: "IS THERE A CORE LIMITING BELIEF THAT GOES WITH THIS? WHAT IS MY DEEPEST KNOWING ABOUT THIS BELIEF?"

If a contraction does not start to soften or unfold via the prior steps, it's almost always because a core belief is holding it in place. This is the right time to pose the above question. Again, we bring attention to the heart area, drop in this question, and listen without going to the mind for an answer.

Our process of awakening and unfolding
does not proceed in neat linear stages.

Core limiting beliefs, whether sub- or semiconscious, have enormous power and can often be reduced to short, simple sentences such as *I am worthless. I am unlovable. I am lacking. I am flawed.* You can also recognize them because they induce an emotional reaction and palpable somatic contraction.

I'll review this subject in detail in the next chapter, offering examples of how it works. All conditioning is a complex of thought, feeling, and sensation, and beliefs are often the lynchpin that holds these complexes together. Being able to detect and effectively question our core limiting beliefs is one of the most important things we can do to support the recognition and embodiment of our true nature.

LET IN THE SHIFT AND THE UNDERSTANDING

You might have noticed that this last step is identical to the one I presented with the meditative inquiry instructions. It's not enough to be temporarily relieved from our emotional and mental discomfort—we need to learn from it and let it wake us up. All of our mental, emotional, and somatic reactions are wake-up calls, little alarm bells that let us know that we are in the grips of ignorance. Take full advantage of these learning experiences. Your body-mind is undergoing a major reorientation toward its true nature. After engaging in a felt-sense exploration and inquiry into a challenging aspect of your conditioning, slow down and let yourself be saturated by the light of awareness.

The Two-Step Dance of Intimacy

Since life is always both still and moving, transcendent and immanent, our process of awakening and unfolding does not proceed along neat linear stages. Sometimes our attention is called to rest as open awareness and sometimes to be intimate with our conditioning. We don't need to fully awaken spiritually before we can consciously attend to our psychological reactivity, nor do we need to clear all of our conditioning (impossible in any case) before we can recognize who we really are.

Each step, whether completely back from or into and through the core of our experience, supports the other. The more anchored in presence we are, the easier it is to be spacious and loving with our reactions. The fewer reactions we have, the easier it is to steadily abide in our true nature as open awareness. This spontaneous movement of attention is a two-step dance of intimacy that supports two essential forms of freedom: the *freedom from* our stories and *freedom to* live and love creatively in our ordinary lives. Both forms of freedom are equally important.

~ *Seven* ~

HEARTFELT INQUIRY
INTO CORE BELIEFS

The only thing worth learning is to unlearn.
The way to do that is to question everything you think you know.
BYRON KATIE, *The Mind at Home with Itself*

IN THE PRIOR CHAPTER I suggested that questioning our core limiting beliefs is one of the most important things we can do to free ourselves from our conditioning. These beliefs about our self—which usually cluster around the themes of being inherently lacking, flawed, or separate—are part of the glue that keeps the delusion of being a separate-self intact. Sometimes these compelling beliefs simply erode on their own, like the pages of a book left out in the sun. There is, however, a powerful complementary approach: we can also see right through these beliefs with the laser-like clarity of heartfelt meditative inquiry.

I recently met with Aaron, a young man I mentor. His account below illustrates how powerful our core beliefs can be and what can happen when we pointedly question them.

> As long as I can remember, there has always been a significant part of me that needed to prove I was lovable. This is what drove me to be a better and different person in other people's eyes in every way imaginable. The basic question was, "Am I lovable, or not?"

John invited me to just sit with the feeling for a while and then to ask the question, "What is my deepest knowing about this?" At first, I was looking for an answer—that I am lovable, worthy of everyone's praise and admiration. It took me a few moments to let go of this and ask the question innocently, without expecting a result.

When I did, I started to experience what I can only describe as a vast emptiness. It was a greater emptiness than anything I had ever experienced, as if everything I had done to control myself and my life was seen through. It was a seeing through of all the ways I thought I could make myself happy, of all the effort to better myself and become somebody else. It felt as if both self-love and self-hatred were irrelevant. Whatever my true nature was, it existed apart from that dimension of thought. I began to feel that I wasn't a "self" at all.

I can't say the experience was pleasurable; it was frightening. John encouraged me to sit with the resistance. There was fear that I wouldn't be able to control my life and of ending up all alone. As we sat with these thoughts, inquiring into the truth of them, I quickly realized that these ways of controlling myself simply don't work. How could I even change myself at all? How would it really help? And how could I possibly know what to change to become happier?

John pointed to a current of life that could be felt in the moment. I then sensed that in this vast emptiness, there was actually something to rely upon, to follow, to trust. We began to laugh about it all. Even on the level of thought, the mind can seem so silly sometimes.

Rather than a dramatic end of suffering or awakening, this was another step in the process of realizing my true nature, of trusting myself.

There are a number of steps that are interesting to unpack here that are relevant to our theme of uncovering the Deep Heart. First, Aaron was able to identify a core belief that had plagued him his whole life. Despite being raised by loving parents, he did not think or feel that he was lovable enough, and he felt compelled to compensate for this apparent lack. As a result, he could never rest as he was. Aaron was always trying to be a different and better self. This is the self-improvement project that few of us are immune to.

Almost everyone struggles or has struggled with an underlying sense of lack, of not being enough in some way. This belief can take various forms. Instead of thinking that we aren't *lovable* enough, we may feel that we are not *worthy* enough. Have you ever secretly believed this? If we are honest with ourselves, we almost always feel like we aren't _____ enough. You can fill in the blank.

Trying to fill in the blank is also an interesting metaphor for how we try to compensate for the nagging sense of deficient emptiness that is inherent when we mistake ourselves to be a separate-self. Our lives are unconsciously driven to try to fill this blank. We see this tendency writ large with narcissism—egocentricity on steroids. The narcissist incessantly craves attention and admiration because this hole can never be filled. Instead of trying to fill a bottomless hole with some form of adulation, we can directly explore this core sense of lack. The true resolution happens when our innocent, curious, and affectionate attention goes into the core of the apparent deficiency.

Once Aaron was able to identify this belief and feel the impact in his body—a contraction in the heart area—I asked him to bring his attention to his heart and to innocently ask himself: *"What is my deepest knowing about this belief?"* Although I encouraged him not to go to his mind for an answer, he did so for a little while, which is completely normal.

When we have a question, we almost always go to our mind for an answer. This is, after all, what the mind is designed for—to recognize patterns, envision possibilities, and solve problems in order to survive. If you observe your thinking carefully for a few minutes, you will see all of these tendencies at work. The fear of survival always lurks in the shadows of an unsolved problem. You can uncover this fear by asking yourself, "What would happen if I don't take care of this problem?" followed up with, "And then what would happen?" multiple times.

The fear of disability or some form of physical or psychological annihilation lies dormant in the psyche's survival basement, ready to be triggered by the smallest possible threat. We are hardwired for hyper-vigilance—what some neuropsychologists call the "negativity bias."[1] This is why catastrophic thinking—the tendency to imagine the worst possible outcome—is so prevalent. We all have some Chicken Little ("The sky is falling!") in us, although it doesn't seem so little when it is triggered.

A clear mind works beautifully when it focuses on solving ordinary problems. For example, if my car doesn't start, I try to figure out the cause so I can fix it: Dead battery? Jumper cables, or maybe have it towed to my mechanic. Am I hungry? If so, I think about where to find my next meal. The mind's *to-do* list is virtually endless.

We can acknowledge our psychological wounds
without viewing them as essential flaws.

The strategic mind is a useful instrument, a true marvel arising from billions of years of evolution. It is capable of discovering some of nature's most profound mysteries—dark matter, quantum entanglement, and how gravity curves the space-time continuum. Not long ago I was marveling at a collection of Michelangelo's drawings, Van Gogh's paintings, and Rodin's sculptures in the Metropolitan Museum of Art in New York. I arrived at the museum by summoning a driver with an app on my smartphone, and I landed in the city a week earlier via the technological magic of modern air travel. It is amazing what the strategic mind can do. However, despite its remarkable capacities, it is severely limited when it comes to intimately investigating our direct subjective experience. A purely analytic, problem-solving mode distracts from self-inquiry. As Adya playfully notes, "We wouldn't ask a hammer about the meaning of life."[2]

Like most of us, Aaron first looked to the problem-solving mind for a reassurance that he was lovable. We all look for reassuring voices, inner and outer, that tell us that our worst doubts and fears are not true. However, this level of psychological reassurance has limited value, as you have probably noticed in your own experience. Analytic under-standing and affirmative self-talk rarely resolve core limiting beliefs and their related feelings and sensations.

This is because core limiting beliefs are almost always based upon some combination of early childhood conditioning and the exis-tential sense of being a separate-self. Although Aaron was treated lovingly as a child, he was not convinced that he was lovable. This is an existential condition shared by people everywhere: We inevitably feel some lack or flaw when we lose touch with our wholeness, but when we consciously rediscover it, this sense of inherent lack or flaw dissolves. Getting back in touch with our wholeness means that we can acknowledge our psychological wounds (which are, more accu-rately, frozen and underdeveloped places) without viewing them as essential flaws.

You are not who you think you are.

Since core limiting beliefs are irrational as well as existential, it is much more effective to access an intuitive form of knowing—heart wisdom—when questioning them. I have experimented for years with how best to evoke this inner knowing, studying various methods of inquiry such as Byron Katie's *The Work* and *The Sedona Method*.[3] These approaches can work beautifully, but I have found that inviting attention into the heart area and then innocently asking, "What is my deepest knowing about this belief?" is the most direct approach. As an alternative, we can also ask ourselves, "What is the truth?" It's a deceptively simple and open process. Something in us (our true nature—which is not really a thing) knows what is true.

When Aaron realized that a mental affirmation of his lovability would not suffice, he stopped looking to his mind for an answer. There was now space for a truly fresh and innocent inquiry. In response, something entirely unexpected arose—the experience of a vast empti-ness, far greater than he had ever felt before. Aaron spontaneously saw through of all of his mind's strategies to create a better version of itself, and a core insight burst forth.

> It felt as if both self-love and self-hatred were irrelevant. Whatever my true nature was, it existed apart from that dimension of thought. I began to feel that I wasn't a "self" at all.

I invite you to take a moment to sit with this stunning revelation: Who you really are—your true nature—is beyond love or hate, affirmation, or negation. It exists beyond any dimension of thought. You are not who you think you are. For Aaron, the ordinary sense of self began to dissolve without being replaced by some different or higher self, and he realized that he was no self at all. This is a common description of what it feels like to be undefined by any image or story. For Aaron, it was an initially unpleasant and frightening realization.

This is completely understandable. It was frightening to Aaron because he clearly saw that he was not in control. This is terrifying for the mind—its entire job is to be in control (or at least to imagine it is). Aaron's primal fear was of being unable to control whether others would love him, and if he couldn't do that, it would mean ending up all alone. Almost all of us carry this primal fear of abandonment. Modern humans have been around—mostly in small groups of hunters and gatherers—for several hundred thousand years. As a result, our psychology and morality is fundamentally tribal. Until relatively recently, being alone for a human meant being cast out of the tribe, which would result in almost certain death.

Aaron's process of inquiry, however, continued: Could he change himself? Would such a change bring safety? How would he even know what to change? The ground of his self-construction and self-improvement project was completely falling away as he saw its futility. How would he be able to navigate his life if there was no self? The simple answer is: quite beautifully! Yet, Aaron's ordinary mind did not have a clue how this could happen. Of course, he was afraid.

At this juncture I pointed out an underlying current of life that exists within this apparent emptiness of self-definition. This isn't an abstract idea, but a palpable felt sense of something in the core of our being that is quietly running the show. Aaron was able to immediately sense into it. When he did, his fear fell away.

As we learn to tap into the interior of our body and inhabit it, we can sense a subtle current of aliveness that runs vertically through the core. It feels like a clear, luminous line of energy that runs upward close to the spine. It seems to well up from the ground like a pure spring and feels as if it radiates high above our head. If you imagine that your body is suspended in midair by a fine line located at the top of your head, you may get a sense of it.

I call it the current of life because it contains an essential aliveness and intelligence. Tibetan Buddhists refer to this as the *central channel*, and Hindu yogis call it the *sushumna*. It may sound esoteric, but the current of life exists within each of us like the fine filament of an incandescent bulb. The fewer filters we have—limiting beliefs, emotional reactions, and somatic contractions—the easier it is to sense this core animating luminosity.

As we awaken to our true nature, attention naturally drops down and into the interior of the body. The ability to sense this varies among individuals, but the hallmark of attuning with this life current is the sense of being deeply at home within oneself—centered in the core of one's being and aligned with something much greater than the little *me*.

Aaron could easily sense this life current when I pointed it out to him. The question of whether he would be able to navigate life without his ordinary approval-seeking identity became laughable, and he felt an immediate sense of trust.

What Is a Core Limiting Belief, and How Do I Recognize It?

In the closing circle of a recent retreat, a delightful woman in her early sixties shared what had touched her the most. She admitted that she had attended the retreat mostly to be closer to her daughter (who was also a participant), but what struck her most was that she had never realized how much her entire life had been ruled by a core limiting belief. She confessed that she never knew that such a thing even existed. Seeing her belief and beginning to feel some space from it was a liberating revelation for her, and she was delighted to come out of a box that she didn't know she had put herself in for most of her life.

It's like that for most of us. Core limiting beliefs form in childhood and mostly reside outside or on the edge of conscious awareness. They are *core* in the sense that everything about us organizes around them—how we relate to others, work, and take care of ourselves. They are *limiting* because they constrain us, holding us back from living our lives as wakefully, freely, wisely, powerfully, joyfully, lovingly, and creatively as we can.

Beliefs are mental maps—approximations of reality. They help orient us, and most are benign. Generally, the closer they correspond to facts, the more useful they are. Of course, some nonfact-based beliefs provide solace and meaning in the face of existential uncertainty—for example, the desire for a pleasant afterlife somewhere up in the fluffy clouds or in a celestial desert oasis.

Core limiting beliefs are particularly powerful lenses through which we see ourselves and the world. Our view of the world always has a corresponding view of our self. If we see the world as a hostile and dangerous place, we will also believe that we need to either armor or conceal ourselves in order to survive—becoming aggressive or invisible depending on our temperament and conditioning. Conversely, if we perceive the world as friendly, we will feel safe to let down our guard, come out of hiding, and shine just as we are.

Core limiting beliefs about our self can be stated in short, simple, and childlike sentences. A few examples include *I am not good enough, I am worthless, something is wrong with me, I don't deserve to exist, I am a mistake, I'm bad, I'm flawed, I am broken and beyond repair, I'm unlovable,* and *I don't belong.* There are endless variations on these basic themes, and it's important that we recognize the *specific* form that they take in our own lives. For example, *I'm flawed* may take the form of *I'm really screwed up* (or something more vulgar) particularly suited to our family and culture. You can tell that you have correctly identified one of these beliefs when it evokes a strong emotional charge and contraction in your body.

This happens because our core beliefs are a complex of semi- or sub-conscious thoughts with accompanying feelings and sensations. When I work with groups, I sometimes invite participants to try the following brief, unpleasant experiment.

> Take a moment to reflect on a compelling core limiting belief that you have about yourself. Keep it as short and simple as possible, using the language of a child. You won't need to disclose it to anyone. Experiment with different variations until you find the form with the most charge. Once you have found it, notice the impact emotionally and somatically. Observe it carefully for a little while and note that it is caused by your thinking. Take a deep breath and let it go.

I then ask group members who are willing to share the impact of their core limiting beliefs without necessarily disclosing the belief itself. I frame the invitation this way because there is often tremendous shame associated with these beliefs. Invariably people report unpleasant feelings such as shame and fear along with sensations of gripping or freezing in the interior of their body—somatic contractions. Core limiting beliefs induce a shutting down and pulling in—an inner collapsing, gripping, and armoring. The stronger the belief, the greater the impact.

It may help to do this experiment by writing down a list of your top five "hits" and then narrowing your list down to one or two that seem most central. Try it now. Pick the belief with the most impact. It may seem strange or unpleasant, but keep in mind that these highly confining beliefs with their attendant emotional and somatic reactions are also entry points for discovering your fundamental nature, and they can work like keys to unlock the depths of your heart.

Some people find that speaking these beliefs out loud with a trusted friend or therapist helps them to identify which ones have the most charge. During the process of heartfelt meditative inquiry, which I will describe shortly, these beliefs may also further clarify or even dissolve to be replaced by ones that are closer to the core. When this happens, we simply continue with the inquiry. We discover and see through each layer with increasing clarity.

When people start to attune with their heart,
they report a sense of homecoming.

Another way to recognize a core belief is to focus attention on a familiar emotional reaction—shame or fear, for example—or a somatic contraction, such as a knot in the solar plexus or the heart area. Take a few minutes to simply feel the feeling and sense the sensation as it is without trying to change it. Then ask yourself: "Is there a belief that goes with this?" Be quiet and wait, trying not to grasp with your mind for an answer. Usually the belief will bubble up quickly. Whichever approach you take to recognizing your core limiting beliefs—asking yourself directly, making a list, or starting with reactive feelings and sensations—you are learning how to look under the hood of your conditioning to discover the patterns that drive you. It's a crucial step in freeing yourself from illusion.

How Do I Question a Core Belief?

Once you have recognized a core limiting belief, attune with your heart wisdom to question it. First, drop your attention from the head to the heart area.

It may help to put your hand over the center of your chest and imagine that you can inhale and exhale directly from this area. Take a minute to quietly attune. You are signaling a willingness to listen in a different way and are also entering into silent contact with your true nature as loving awareness. Poetically speaking, you are summoning your highest muse—heart wisdom, a blend of nonjudgmental clarity and loving-kindness that is always available.

You can sense when your attention shifts from your head to the heart. It's as if your center of gravity drops down like a descending elevator into your midchest. Not only are you feeling into the heart, you are starting to take up residence there. You may sense a feeling of warmth, openness, and intimacy. When people start to attune with their heart, they report a sense of homecoming and often feel closer to themselves. When I sit with people who are finding their way home, I can feel a radiant glow in my heart area, which happens because we all share the same home as loving awareness.

It can take a minute or two for this shift to happen. Take your time. With practice, it can occur in seconds. Once it feels like your attention is grounded in the heart area, you are ready for the next step:

Ask yourself: "What is my deepest knowing about this belief?" Don't go to your mind for an answer.

If your belief is that you are not good enough, for example, state your question like this: "What is my deepest knowing about this belief that I am not good enough?" Use the exact language that you have used to formulate the belief. The clearer your question is, the more precise the response will be.

I know that I am being repetitious, but there is a reason that I keep reminding you to not go to your mind for an answer. Going to ordinary thinking is the single most common way to sabotage your inquiry. When you are willing to not know with your problem-solving, strategic mind, a different and more essential form of knowing becomes possible.

There is no right answer in this inquiry. In fact, there is no "answer" as such. Instead, we are inviting a holistic response. One of my reservations about Byron Katie's "Work" (which I greatly appreciate in general) is that the first two questions in her protocol—"Is it true" and "Can you absolutely know that it is true?"—are binary. You can only answer yes or no, and you know beforehand that the correct answer is always no. Framing the inquiry this way tends to keep attention localized in the mind.

Once we have clearly formulated a core belief, shifted our attention from the head to the heart, and then inquired into our heartfelt knowing, we let the question go, wait, feel, and listen. A response can come in any form. For example, when I inquire in this way, a response often comes first as a subtle sensation in the interior of my body. It's as if something lights up inside. As I sit with this subtle sensation, letting it be with openness and curiosity, a word or image will usually arise to accompany it. It's as if a pearl begins to materialize on the ocean floor, readying itself to be brought up to the surface by a deep-sea diver. I will check to see and feel if the arising word or image resonates with the original sensation, and it takes clearer shape as I do so. Sharing it with another person also brings it out from the private into the public domain, which makes the response even more potent.

This process of discovery varies from person to person. For some, a word or an image will immediately appear with or without any sensation. Others will experience a silent knowing of the complete irrelevance of their belief. As described earlier, Aaron had a sudden and clear realization that his true nature was beyond any judgments, good or bad. The point is to discover how a response comes to you and then honor it. We honor our responses by consciously letting them in as gifts from the gods and then acting upon them. This deep dive into our inner knowing and re-immersion with a new, liberating understanding directly parallels what mythologist Joseph Campbell described as the hero's (or heroine's) journey.[4]

"I Am All Alone"

In a recent meeting, Carolyn described feeling radiant and in touch with her true nature when she was in a "field of love" meeting with certain people: me, her piano teacher, her singing teacher, her yoga teacher, her acupuncturist, and sometimes when she was alone in her garden or in nature in the mornings. She described these encounters as beads strung along a necklace with the spaces in between as interstices. We then had the following conversation that included a period of heartfelt inquiry, and I questioned the reality of these apparent in-between spaces that she was experiencing:

> **Carolyn**   I guess I won't feel this [field of love]
> all the time unless I have a full-blown awakening.

> **John**   Carolyn, there are no interstices other
> than in your mind.

I get out of my chair and open the door of my room to the office hallway.

John   Is the space outside my office less full than
the space inside?

Carolyn   Yes, it is (laughing)! No, of course not.
It is all in my mind.

John   So, what is the story that you are telling yourself
that makes you feel as if there are these gaps in the field
of love?

Carolyn (sits quietly for a little while)   That I will
always be alone. No, that I *am* alone.

John   I invite you to bring your attention to the heart
area and ask yourself, "What is your deepest knowing
about this belief?"

She closes her eyes and sits with this question in silence for about two
minutes. I feel a shift happening in her heart area. Visually, she also
looks brighter. She opens her eyes, beaming.

Carolyn   The truth is that I am surrounded and
saturated by this field of love. When I acknowledged
this, it felt as if these dark talons or claws are released
from my heart.

John   Let this in.

Carolyn   This love feels unconditional, like Christ's
love. All the parts within me that feel flawed and
unworthy are fully embraced by this love.

She now looked and felt radiant, clear, and full, and her eyes brimmed
with gratitude.

It was fascinating to see that Carolyn's ability to know herself in and as a field of unconditional love was so easily accessible when she was with one of her teachers or healers and yet so hard to find on her own (other than when she gardened or was in nature in the morning). To her, life felt like a beaded necklace—filled with jewels of loving contact and presence, but also with significant painful gaps. Perhaps you have also felt this way—alive and fulfilled when you are with family, friends, or a beloved teacher, but bereft when you are by yourself.

In Carolyn's case, the underlying obstacle was the unexamined belief that she was alone in some essential way. The effect of this belief was a contraction in the heart area that appeared as dark talons. When she saw through her belief, the talons released, and she felt herself immersed in unconditional love, embraced just as she was. The interstices disappeared; the gaps closed. She did not doubt that she *was* this love.

Protocol for Heartfelt Inquiry into Core Beliefs

1. Identify a core limiting belief. Keep it short and note its emotional and somatic charge. Then let it go.

2. Shift your attention from the head to the heart area.

3. Ask yourself: "What is my deepest knowing about this belief?"

4. Don't go to your mind for an answer. Be quiet. Listen, feel, and sense. A response can come in any form.

5. Let it in.

~ *Eight* ~

NOT KNOWING AND THE AWAKENING OF THE DEEP HEART

Abide in the heart, not knowing.
JEAN KLEIN, Corte Madera, 1988

WHEN AARON QUESTIONED his story that he was unlovable, he encountered a vast emptiness that was completely new to him. He then recognized a current of life radiating in the core of his being. When Carolyn slowed down enough to question her underlying assumption that she was essentially alone, she discovered that she was immersed in and embraced by a field of love that was not separate from her and that did not depend upon being with others. These discoveries were enlightening and enlivening; both Aaron and Carolyn felt lit up internally and filled with a sense of aliveness. Their sense of delight was contagious. Of course, it may take time for these insights to fully bloom in their day-to-day lives, but neither of them doubted the reality and importance of what they had discovered.

You might believe that these kinds of essential discoveries are rare or hard to come by. If you are holding that story, I invite you to let it go. We just need to know where and how to look—into our heart and our true nature as loving awareness, and with the natural curiosity, affection, and innocence to be found there.

We must first be willing to see the limits
of the ordinary mind and give up the illusion
of being in complete control of our life.

I often share the epigraph to this chapter—*Abide in the heart, not knowing*—with my students. Jean Klein said that to me over thirty years ago in a personal interview, and the aphorism points beautifully to how we can avail ourselves to our true nature. It invites us to listen in a completely new way, centering our attention in the heart area without any conclusion or goal.

When we do this, we will at some point discover that we are the listening itself and not the objects—the thoughts, feelings, and sensations—of our listening. The nature of this listening is pure, all-inclusive, open awareness. No one is open; there is just openness. As we abide more intimately *in* the heart, we will discover that we *are* the Heart of awareness that is not essentially separate from anyone or anything. It is a radically simple discovery. What has been true all along becomes obvious, even if this recognition astonishes the ordinary mind that thinks and perceives that everything is separate.

Don't Know, Can't Know, Don't Need to Know

If our attention is to abide or rest in the heart, we must first be willing to see the limits of the ordinary mind and give up the illusion of being in complete control of our life. There's a great deal that the mind does not know. The purpose of the ordinary, strategic mind is to try to know in order to assume control, and—to a certain degree—it works. For example, the more we can know about an environment, process, or a person, the more reliably we can direct outcomes. The scientific method is based on formulating clear hypotheses, making careful observations, performing rigorous testing, and repeatedly verifying results. Our rapid technological progress relies on this. However, by itself, this approach to life does not bring individual or collective happiness, as the proliferation of weapons of mass destruction, climate disruption, and growing income disparity will attest. Rational thinking is useful, but insufficient. In order to apply our relative knowledge wisely, we must turn to another source for guidance.

The ordinary mind is a good servant but a poor master. When it doesn't know its limits, it easily becomes a misguided, arrogant tyrant. Traditional European monarchies appointed regents or stewards whenever an heir to the throne was too young to assume the responsibilities of being the king or queen. When the heir came of age, regents were expected to end their stewardships and hand over their authority. In a few cases, however, regents refused to surrender their power, having become enamored with it, and crises ensued. This is a telling metaphor for what happens when the ordinary mind assumes more authority than it is designed to wield. It's not enough to be clear and rational. We also need to be wise and loving.

When we step back and reflect a little, we can easily see that our ordinary, strategic mind knows relatively little. We don't know what will happen in the next moment or even what our next thought will be, and most of our lives are wildly different from what we imagined them to be. At the moment, I am writing in my French sister-in-law's home an hour north of Paris—I could never have predicted such a thing until quite recently. We don't know the time of our death, what successes or failures await us in the days ahead, or what friends and partners we will gain and lose. The truth is that the course of our life is unknown. We may have occasional intuitions of possibility, but little more, and there isn't much we can do about it. More importantly, there isn't anything we need to do about it!

Who we really are is not something
we can define or confine with thought.

It is enough that we listen and follow moment to moment. It is enough that we are open, are available, and take the next obvious step and see what happens. It is enough when the ordinary mind bows down to the wisdom of the heart and trusts the movement of a wiser current. When we surrender to it, a natural authority in the core of our being guides our life quite beautifully.

One of the first Korean Zen masters to come to the United States was Seung Sahn. He repaired washing machines for a few years before becoming established in the West—an unexpected twist in his life, I'm sure. I used to attend his dharma talks in Berkeley in the mid-1980s when he was traveling through the Bay Area. One of his main teachings was "Only don't know."[1] During his dialogues with students, he would often interrupt them when he felt they were becoming too heady, playfully make a growling sound, and then threaten them in his simple English: "I hit you with stick! Only don't know mind, go straight ahead!" The questioner and other audience members would laugh. Seung Sahn's point was that we overly rely on our thinking minds to try to understand what is essential.

Not knowing refers not only to our inability to know what will happen; it also means that we cannot know our true nature solely by thinking about it. Who we really are is not something we can define or confine with thought. Who we really are is quite literally inconceivable and unimaginable. Our true nature is not an object—it exists prior to the mind. We can say what our true nature is *not*, at least initially, but we cannot definitively state what it *is*. Yet we can know it directly by consciously being it. When the mind clearly recognizes that it is not going to understand what is prior to it, a spontaneous letting go occurs, and attention quite naturally rests in the heart.

Is There a Problem Right Now?

As we have seen, the mind is highly oriented to problem solving, so much so that if there isn't an actual pending problem, it will invent one to solve! Certainly there are challenging situations that require our careful attention and action, but a problem is usually a story about an impending catastrophe. Asking yourself whether or not you're facing a true problem *right now* has a way of disarming the mind. It invites the mind to stand down from its familiar hypervigilance and to allow attention to fall into the heart. This inquiry can be helpful when you first sit to meditate.

Essential knowing is not limited to or by the body.

I posed this question during a retreat last year, and one woman, after wrestling with it for a day, reported her process to the group. At first she resented the question. Her adult daughter had struggled with a life-threatening illness for much of her life, and the woman worried daily about her daughter's health—*of course* there was *always* a problem. Upon reflection, however, she realized that her daughter no longer approached her own life from this perspective and had learned to live in the present moment, grateful for the life that she had. If her daughter could live with this freedom, the mother realized that she had permission to do so as well.

Deeper Dimensions of the Heart

As we learn to abide in the heart not knowing, a different kind of knowing appears. It speaks in a different voice, one that does not judge, assert, insist, or deny. Amidst the cacophony of the mind's stream of thoughts, the voice of heart-wisdom is more like a murmur—the quiet guest at the noisy dinner table of daily life. This knowing may use words or images, or it may be immediate, direct, and unmediated by language or imagery. It may come as a subtle feeling and sensation—a glow of recognition when the truth is spoken, an inner sense of illumination. Or it may use all of these modes in combination like a symphony.

The body-mind is a conduit *for* (rather than the ultimate source *of*) this knowing. Certainly, there is a wisdom of the body, but essential knowing is not limited to or by the body. Although we primarily sense this knowing in the heart and the belly, it is not confined to these areas. Sages teach that this loving awareness is independent of all circumstances and precedes the coming and going of all experience, even as it is intimate with all experience. Whether we believe that this quiet, clear, and loving awareness exists as a transcendent field or is a byproduct of the body-mind, we can experience it directly and benefit by connecting with it. This is not a matter of faith, but of attunement.

In chapter 2, I offered a three-dimensional map of the heart as a continuum—a wave tip, wave base, and ocean. To review, these correspond with the ego identity, soul, and Self (or no-self). The tip is at the surface of the heart area in the center of the chest, the base of the wave is at the very back of the heart area, and the ocean is the infinite space within, behind and around the body. Discovering and opening the heart is a movement of diving in and falling back.

I can feel this when I sit with people, as can they. The further they go in their process of discovery, the further back attention drops into the heart area. It's as if the heart is a tunnel with increasingly subtle depth that corresponds with a subjective sense of illumination, expansion, and intimacy. As this happens, it feels like they are getting to "the heart of the matter," whatever it may be. For example, if my clients or students are exploring grief, they shed various stories of being abandoned and unworthy until they experience the raw sensation of pure loss. The capacity to allow grief also makes space for joy to emerge.

This exploration is not always pleasant or easy. At times, it can be emotionally painful, as well as threatening to our conventional sense of self. There are myriad conscious and unconscious reasons why we distract ourselves from this journey into heart. We put up walls that we're not even conscious of in order to bury our pain and ensure that we are not hurt again. We then identify with these self-imposed prison cells and think and feel that they define us—that we are small, deficient, and separate. We pay a severe price by isolating ourselves, feeling rigid, exhausted, fragile, cut-off, and half-alive. Is this why zombies have become such a popular and terrifying image in our culture these days?

The Subtle Heart on the Right

When we explore the heart area, the movement of attention is a vertical descent, like a diver who plumbs the depths of the ocean. The further down we go, the more essential the discovery will be. There is a subtle energetic dimension of the Deep Heart that often remains hidden—a sea cave, if you will. It's the heart on the right side of the chest.

When I first read a small book in the late 1970s on the teachings of Ramana Maharshi, the great south Indian sage, I was drawn by his luminous eyes but understood very little of his teachings. I did not have a feel for his main method of inquiry, which was to ask oneself, "Who am I?" Nor did I understand his teachings about the Heart. According to Ramana, while the Heart, or pure consciousness, was ultimately nonlocatable, there was also a "Heart on the right side" that was "two finger-breadths" to the right of midchest from which the "I-thought" arose.[2]

It was only ten years later, after being exposed to self-inquiry through Nisargadatta Maharaj's teachings and spending time with Jean Klein, that I began to spontaneously sense this subtle center on the right. For years, often in the middle of the night, it felt like this area was being drilled through with a diamond lathe or operated upon by an unseen surgeon with a laser. Although this spontaneous process was arduous, I knew it was benevolent. When the opening was clear, the drilling ended. I associate the heart on the right side with a feeling of profound surrender and infinite gratitude. When my attention is not engaged with a project, it now naturally rests here.

Psychodynamic and Existential Levels

As I follow my clients' and students' journeys, I am often reminded of Joseph Campbell's description of the archetypal hero's or heroine's journey, where someone feels an inner call, resists it, gets support from a mentor, plunges into an underworld, encounters obstacles, discovers treasures, and returns to enrich the community. Dreams and various myths around the world are often filled with these motifs.

The first obstacles that we encounter in this inner journey are usually psychodynamic in origin. They arise from the psychological conditioning we experienced in our families of origin. Further explorations unearth earlier imprints, and resistance to uncovering this conditioning is correspondingly strong, which makes sense. If we were neglected, abandoned, or abused on a primal level, we would not want to experience these unbearable, destabilizing feelings again. Who wants to feel terrified, disconnected, unworthy, and ashamed?

This domain, of course, is the core focus of depth psychotherapy. Some people need to engage in therapy in order to find healthy relationships and meaningful work. No amount of meditation, self-inquiry, satsangs, or retreats will replace the slow, attuned, and one-on-one relational work designed to repair these early ruptures, undo traumatic impacts, and foster emotional maturity. Spiritual teachers who do not have firsthand experience with relational and traumatic disruptions or who have not addressed them within themselves often have difficulty understanding this level of conditioning. They would do well to learn when to refer some of their struggling students to mature, skilled psychotherapists for the kind of attention that lies outside of their expertise. Additionally, Westerners raised in less cohesive cultures and families tend to have different psychological needs than their Eastern brethren, and it's often the case that Eastern contemplative traditions are less adapted to meet developmental needs of this type.

As I suggested in an earlier chapter, the unfolding of the Deep Heart and our true nature does not happen in a neat, linear fashion. At times our attention will be drawn to pure presence and other times to our conditioning. Generally speaking, as our psychodynamic conditioning resolves, existential dimensions of experience emerge. It's as if the psychological blockages in the heart tunnel soften or dissolve (imagine rubble clearing), allowing for a clearer path to emerge.

By "existential dimension" I mean that which we all share as human beings, regardless of our specific psychological conditioning. Attention moves from the unique conditioning that we have endured as a wave-tip individual to those conditions that all individual waves experience: biological survival, dealing with impermanence, finding purpose and meaningful work in the world, entering into intimate relationships with others, being authentic, experiencing aloneness and separateness, gaining self-knowledge, and awakening to who we really are. These are the inescapable challenges and opportunities of being human.

Letting go comes from clear seeing.

Psychotherapists tend to hunt for the origins of suffering solely in psychological conditioning. This is a significant mistake. The other evening I was speaking with Jeroen, a Dutch friend and mentee, who's been training to be a Hakomi therapist. He described one of his training seminars in which he was in the role of the client exploring a residual feeling, sensation, and belief that he did not fit in this world. His training partner, who was a psychotherapist, wanted to find the origin of this feeling in Jeroen's childhood. This did not feel completely right to Jeroen.

As Jeroen and I sat with his experience, exploring it more intimately, he could remember being three years old and feeling a sense of separation that had nothing to do with his family. A feeling of primordial aloneness arose that he associated with the image of a wandering monk who was "alone, not belonging to anything or anyone, connected with everything yet not completely grounded or having arrived in the world." After a short period of sitting with his deepest knowing about this belief and feeling, he felt a sense of release, accompanied with sensations of wholeness, peace, groundedness, and a strong flow of life energy. The light of his well-established inner knowing, based on years of contemplation, meditation, and self-inquiry, softened and melted these icy remains of aloneness. Jeroen clearly saw through an existential residue of separateness that had nothing to do with his familial conditioning. The letting go was a natural byproduct of his clarity—his ability to see through something that was not true.

This last point is critically important. Letting go comes from clear seeing. A true letting go can never be forced. Rather, it's a spontaneous result of in-depth understanding. This is why the path of self-recognition is so transformative. When we see through an illusion, it no longer has power over us, just as when we realize that we cannot quench our thirst with a dry well. When Jeroen recognized that there was no one to fit into anything and nothing to fit into, the old complex of thought, feeling, and sensation dissolved. The fist of confusion relaxed, and an open hand, filled with aliveness and gratitude, appeared.

In Jeroen's case, the heart area was only indirectly involved. His issue was not about feeling unworthy or unloved but rather about not belonging, which centered more in his solar plexus. He came to a global sense of awareness through a different door. Nevertheless, the sense of spacious, vibrant, affectionate awareness that arose for him was the same that others experience via the heart area. All doors lead to the same destination—that same sense of coming home to oneself.

I mentioned earlier that core limiting beliefs can have both psycho-dynamic (early childhood conditioning) and existential dimensions. As we work through these and their related emotional reactions and somatic contractions, the deepest level of the human heart becomes illumined and consciously available. We arrive at the core of the localized human heart that can be sensed as a point of subtle energy and light at the back of the heart area.

The Back of the Heart

For me, the word *soul* is a poetic formulation. I can't assert that the back of the heart is where some separate entity resides that migrates between lifetimes or goes on to higher levels after the death of the body. I also cannot rule this out; I really don't know. Even if there is some subtle individual stream of conditioning and learning that continues across lifetimes—a so-called *mind-stream*—at some point this stream will dissolve into the ocean, the beautiful destiny of all rivers.

When our attention rests at the back of the heart, we are on the border of the impersonal and the personal. Here the universal field of loving awareness starts to take form as an individual. The ocean begins to take shape as a unique wave with the differentiated flavors, colors, and tones of an individual being. When we are consciously in touch with this level, we have the sense of being fully alive. We feel more aligned with a current of life and act increasingly in accord with it, and our life feels intrinsically meaningful, no matter what we are doing.

What we do has an archetypal feeling to it, as if greater forces are at work through us. We experience a sense of flow. Our work feels inspired, regardless of its impact on others, and offerings from this level often touch others in profound ways, even if they are expressed through small, random acts of insight, kindness, generosity, and gratitude.

Essential qualities pour through us. If we are an artist, we find ourselves freely perceiving and sharing beauty. If we are a teacher, we inspire others to discover and learn. If we are a leader, we are naturally inclined to serve the common good and empower others. If we are a warrior, we courageously protect those who cannot protect themselves. If we are a nurturer, our attuned love and kindness soothes, nourishes, and uplifts. If we are a healer, we foster health and integration in powerful ways. We can play various archetypal roles and express essential qualities at different times, sometimes simultaneously. Life can move through us in surprising ways, and we feel *well used*. Most of us have experienced this at some time, even briefly, in our lives.

When we know our self as the ocean,
we can see waves for what they are.

On a relational level, the love that springs forth feels particularly pure and sweet. When friends or lovers share on this level, it is intoxicating. It's as if two distinct musical instruments harmonize with one another, as in an exquisite duet between a cello and violin. We enjoy a shared sense of seeing and being seen on a profound level.

That being said, there are two significant traps to be aware of, especially given the potent and alluring quality of experiences one can have here. The first is narcissistic inflation, and the second is to mistake the essential qualities of this level as the goal of the spiritual quest. In the first trap, we overidentify with these roles or energies—for example, we may think we are the only or most talented artist, teacher, leader, prophet, healer, warrior, lover, or human being walking on the planet. We may imagine that we are the Chosen One, that we have a cosmic mission, and therefore believe we deserve special treatment and attention. The point of this inflation is to be admired and to have our value recognized by others. If we are honest, almost all of us can detect at least minor currents of this desire to be recognized in our day-to-day life. If we lack psychological insight or spiritual maturity, it can easily seduce us.

The tendency to inflate and feel superior compensates for an underlying sense of lack that always accompanies the sense of being a separate-self. The greatest antidote to inflation is to recognize our true nature. Potent energies and powerful roles may come and go, appear and disappear, but when we know our fundamental nature as open, wakeful, loving awareness, we neither attach to nor identify with these passing states and roles. When we know our self as the ocean, we can see waves for what they are—even the big ones.

The second trap mentioned above is to think that we have reached the goal of our quest. These essential qualities, beautiful as they are, are byproducts of self-recognition. They emerge spontaneously from the source and are not ultimately separate from it, but they are not the source itself. Synchronicities are fun, flow states are potent, and expansive states can be ecstatic, but they all pass. Who we are fundamentally does not come and go. Our true nature is always here as the source and substance of whatever we experience, whether or not those experiences are expansive or pleasant. Knowing this lets us enjoy these states and qualities without becoming overly attached to or identified with them.

Awakening to the Great Heart

Beyond archetypes and essential qualities lies the Great Heart of awareness. When we tap into this, we know that we are whole and not separate from anyone or anything, and we know that this is true of everyone, whether they realize it or not. This recognition does not make us special; it releases us from the need to be special. Love is unconditional. There are no strings attached and no bargains to make. Further, the scope of this love is all-embracing—it is the only thing that holds the individual and collective suffering of humanity.

As the Great Heart opens, we sense the suffering of others more acutely, even as our own suffering resolves. There is an extraordinary amount of suffering in this world that is too much for any individual to bear, no matter how caring and compassionate they may be. When we discover the Great or Universal Heart (sometimes associated with the archetype of the Great Mother), we can experience a sense of discovering That Which Holds It All. If you take the time to quietly sit and contemplate it, Michelangelo's *Pietà* in St. Peter's Cathedral in the Vatican conveys this feeling.

When the Great Heart awakens, we feel a compelling sense that all is well no matter what. We feel our self at rest in our home ground, intimate with all things, but this intimacy is not personal. Strange as it may seem, the greatest intimacy is the least personal. When this is known and felt, the heart has awakened to its true nature.

I did not know this for much of my life. In my case, the process of self-recognition has been gradual. I've studied and practiced for decades with occasional openings, and all of them were catalyzed by my teachers. The image of a slow, steady river with a few waterfalls comes to mind. While this process of awakening seemed to be personal as it unfolded—that is, it seemed to be happening to *me*—this no longer feels true. What is known doesn't refer to or belong to anyone, no more than the ocean refers to or belongs to a particular river.

My first glimpse of this infinite domain of awareness came while I was with Jean Klein on retreat in 1987. One night during a dialogue, it felt as if a subtle center of observation in my head—a mental *me* that had always been there—imploded. Jean sensed this and advised me to be silent. I went to bed a little later, quickly feel asleep, and when I awoke a few hours later, I could no longer locate myself as a separate entity. Instead, I knew that I was infinite awareness. This experience lasted until I began to interact with people in the morning, which evoked a familiar sense of being a separate-self. Jean sat down across from me at breakfast and, with a twinkle in his eye, said, "It was a very interesting night, wasn't it?" Somehow he knew what had happened. Although I had briefly glimpsed who I really was, I also knew that I could not willfully recreate or hold onto it.

Years later, I was on my first residential retreat in 2001 with Adya outside of Lone Pine, California. During a dialogue on the last night, I heard a surprisingly clear inner voice and reported it to Adya:

John   There's a little voice inside of me saying, "Finish me off."

Adya   What's not finished?

John   I don't know.

Adya   Then you are finished.

As Adya looked into my eyes, I had the distinct sense that I was look-ing into the eyes of Infinity. A moment later, I also realized that the Infinite was also looking out through my eyes. It felt as if I had been struck with a lightning bolt—the core of my body lit up, and I began to tremble. I fell into silence and continued to sit long after our meet-ing ended. Eventually, I went to bed, and when I awoke in the middle of the night, it smelled as if something outside was burning. There had been a lightning storm, and I wondered if a tree had been hit, but then I realized that some deep-seated residues within my brain were burn-ing like a pile of old tires. When I awoke in the morning, the world was fresh, and I felt a sense of utter clarity and openness.

Six weeks later, I met again with Adya after one of his talks. I asked him if what I had experienced at Lone Pine could be called a mental awakening. He agreed, but added matter-of-factly, "Let the same thing that happened here (gesturing to his head), happen here (gesturing to his heart area). You already know something about this."

Two years later at a Tibetan retreat center in the Santa Cruz Mountains, Adya gave a talk about the futility of seeking—a theme I had heard both him and Jean address many times before. I became aware that I was still seeking the subtlest of objects—some kind of pure light. As soon as I was honest enough to admit this to myself, I also saw that it was a hopeless venture. In a flash I saw that *seeking* would go on forever—there was no end to it! Suddenly, I realized that I was already whole. It wasn't an intellectual realization; it was a direct and incontrovertible knowing that came as a sudden revelation that I felt in the core of my heart. Later that evening, while walking in the woods, I burst out laughing at how absolutely silly I had been to imagine that I was not already whole. The joke was on me! I was filled with joy. The next day, during a private interview with Adya, I shared my insight. He listened carefully, asked a few checking questions, and then simply said, "I have been waiting for this."

Despite this revelation of essential wholeness, a subtle duality per-sisted—there apparently was a world that was separate from myself. This sense of division resolved two years later while on another retreat with Adya at Mount Madonna, south of Santa Cruz. I was sitting in the garden after dinner contemplating the view of Monterey Bay when it felt as if my head suddenly disappeared, and I saw that everything was made of the same substance as myself. *No one looked out and saw that it was everything.* My jaw literally dropped in astonishment. An open secret revealed itself: Everything that was being seen—the forest, farmlands, and Pacific Ocean in the distance—was made of the same substance as the one who was looking. Everything was consciousness. This recognition vibrated throughout my whole body at the time and, many years later, remains a lively knowing.

I am not suggesting that you will go through these same stages of recognition, first via the mind, then the heart, and then with the apparently separate world. In fact, I am sure that a number of you will not. Those of you who awaken to who you really are, or are engaged somewhere in this process, have a unique path to this recognition. Whatever your path may be, I am confident that you will discover that reality is undivided.

~ *Nine* ~

THE GREAT HEART HOLDS
THE HUMAN HEART

Embrace the wounded heart with the bigger heart.
Let the human heart be found by the heart of being.
ADYASHANTI, *The Revolution of Being*

JULIE WAS ONE of my last supervisees when I taught graduate students at CIIS in San Francisco. After becoming licensed as a psychotherapist, she continued to meet with me for spiritual mentoring. We met a month after Julie gave birth to her first child, a daughter named Lily, and she told me that she had planned to have a home birth with her doula (birth coach) present. However, the birth was arduous, and after nearly thirty-six hours of labor, Julie agreed to go to a nearby hospital. Her doula left unexpectedly. Here's how she later described her birth experience and a subsequent meeting with me:

> When my doula left me, I was so focused and in a no-mind space that I consciously chose to not make up a story that contributed to a sense of separation—a small, poor me that felt abandoned and betrayed. In the moment, there was no interpretation, commentary, or interrupting noise about being left. Instead, I fiercely moved on with my mission of bringing forth life. Emptiness was moving. There was no me who was doing this, but rather something bigger. It

was as if my self moved aside to let something else—that is nothing—move. It felt like grace.

There was another moment at the hospital where everything seemed like it was going downhill. The birth was taking dangerously long, and it was beyond my control. I surrendered to the fact that things might not turn out as I wanted. A split second before my team was about to medically intervene, my baby started to come out naturally. It was another moment of grace. Again, it felt like it wasn't me making it happen but rather allowing life to move through me. This sense of emptiness moving was clear. It was important to experience and understand how there is no need for the small me to function. Things actually work with more ease and flow without it.

A month later, when I shared with John how I wished I could be in that state more often, he pointed out that it was here now. My attention immediately shifted to the background where this emptiness is always present. It is delightful how accessible this always is! As John and I sat together, two facets of truth were very alive: emptiness and fullness. I could feel how the whole dance of life is impersonal. There was a sense of liberation and lightness. I could feel the weight of the separate-self lifting off and a sense of relief.

I could also feel the Big Heart healing my little separate-self heart. The Big Heart is full of love even as there is a sense of nothingness to it. I smiled as I felt into the truth that the Big Heart has room for everything. I could feel how abiding in the True Heart brings a sense of compassion for all of life. I feel deeply grateful. I am not separate. I am loved. I always have been and will always be loved. So is everything and everyone.

In chapter 3 I noted how highly stressful physical and emotional events, as well as unexpected revelations of beauty, can open us to our true nature. Julie was experiencing both at the same time. She was undergoing an extremely stressful birthing experience that could have been exacerbated by her doula's sudden departure, along with the sense of a miraculous unfolding of life. Sometimes it's hard to tell birth and death apart! As an aside, I can recall arriving at my father's deathbed a few minutes after he had died. There was a numinous presence in the room and palpable sense of joy that I had never felt while being with him when he was alive. Life moves in highly mysterious ways to the ordinary mind.

In Julie's case, she experienced the grace of emptiness moving—a paradoxical expression. How can nothing do anything? (Hint: consider the Big Bang.) For Julie, something clearly greater—something that wasn't a thing—had taken over the usual job of the little me. Further, it was doing so with tremendous love, intelligence, and power. While Julie's extraordinary circumstances elicited her clarity and opened her heart, is it possible that this Big Heart is always available regardless of circumstances? When I asked Julie if she could sense it in the moment, she could—with a slight shift of attention to the background.

Can you do the same right now? It's always here, in front of our noses and behind our eyes. We can sense it most clearly when we are out of our mind—not when we are insane, of course, but when we are lucid.

Despite the strong potential to be triggered by her doula's unexpected disappearance, Julie did not indulge her old story of being abandoned and betrayed. She was in a no-mind space, free of the typical self-judgmental commentary that had burdened her in the past. All of her attention was spontaneously focused on the task at hand.

The ocean is never separate from the wave.

Interestingly, her whole experience felt *impersonal*. We generally have negative associations with this word, equating it with coldness, indifference, or the lack of care. Rarely do we associate it with love or warmth. Yet in Julie's case, she felt herself embraced, supported, loved, and healed by a Big Heart that was an impersonal, empty *no-thing*. It is challenging to try to describe an experience that feels so intimate and, at the same time, impersonal. Ordinary language is not adequate.

I felt particularly touched when Julie said that she could also feel the Big Heart healing her little separate-self heart. This was a profound experience for her. Although Julie is a highly sensitive and gifted psychotherapist as well as an ardent lover of essential truth, for years she had felt that there was a gap between her psychological conditioning and her innermost knowing and being. It was as if her childhood fears and her true nature coexisted in different domains. She could feel herself in one or the other, but she could not sense how they were connected. This apparent separation began to dissolve during two retreats she attended while she was pregnant. As this happened, we could sense a hard knot in the heart area softening and opening, along with the feeling of connecting to a global spaciousness and warmth.

This opening between a tight inner contraction and warm spaciousness was accompanied by a growing feeling of love, kindness, and acceptance toward her young self—a self who had felt emotionally abandoned early on. At times this shift included tears and waves of grief. It was as if the light of awareness was tenderly entering into a dark compartment of feeling and subconscious thought that had been sealed for many years in the depths of her heart area. Step-by-step the gap was closing. Unconditioned loving presence was transforming her embedded conditioning. Julie's conscious recognition that she had always been loved—along with everyone and everything else—reflected the Great Heart's embrace of the heart of the little separate-self.

Are there two hearts—a big one and a little one? Not really. It might feel this way at times, but the ocean is never separate from the wave. The Great Heart doesn't reach out to embrace the small heart as a mother might for her lost child; the dissolution of the gap and growing sense of connection with something greater (that is no-thing) is a spontaneous byproduct of seeing things as they truly are. The little separate-self heart is always embraced as it is, whether it knows it or not. When the veil of apparent separation lifts, self-kindness and self-acceptance flourish and radiate out toward oneself and all beings.

While ultimately there are not two hearts, when we are able to make conscious contact with this deeper dimension of loving being, we feel as though we are being held in love and understanding, allowing us to relax. We feel seen as we are. Nothing needs to be fixed or changed. This is the optimal field for psychological healing. If change needs to happen, it will on its own.

Sometimes this sense of being held by a greater field of loving awareness happens when we are alone. It can feel as if it wells up from the core of our being. Other times it feels as if we are enveloped by it from the outside. These different ways of experiencing reflect the immanent and transcendent nature of this awareness that is both within and beyond all experience.

Often we have a taste of it when we are in the loving presence of another person, someone who both sees and loves us as we are. When this happens, the field of the Great Heart is being consciously expressed through a specific individual. Parents often feel this for their children; conscious friends and partners can offer this for one another, as can teachers and their students. The practice below gives you a way to start sensing into this on your own:

MEDITATION
Feel Yourself Being Held

Find a quiet place where you won't be disturbed for a few minutes, sit comfortably upright, and close your eyes or lower them partially. Allow at least a minute to experience each of the following steps, pausing between each of them. Take as long as you'd like with the final step.

1. Take a few deep, slow breaths, sensing your lower belly, and relax.

2. Feel the weight of your body held by whatever you are sitting on. Then sense how the earth's gravity is holding your body.

3. Let your exhalation completely empty into the earth. Wait for the inhalation to come on its own.

4. Feel yourself held by something greater and relax into it. Let yourself be held.

5. Sense into your heart area and feel that you are seen and loved just as you are.

6. Be one with this field of loving awareness.

This simple practice reorients your nervous system to the present experience of being held, as well as your heart to being loved as you are. Try this for two weeks in the mornings and notice how your experience of life changes.

~

It's usually not enough that we are loved because of our role as a family member, lover, or friend. On some level, we also need to know that we are clearly and uniquely loved; we need to feel seen and felt in an attuned way. Infants crave this quality of attention and will have emotional meltdowns when it is even briefly withheld by their mother. We thrive when we feel it as adults. The Deep Heart blossoms when it is recognized by another, regardless of our age.

The Wounded Heart

We are continuing to learn more about the origins and impacts of childhood conditioning, particularly when it comes to developmental trauma. Researchers have discovered that children respond differently to traumatic events than adults do.[1] In part this is due to their undeveloped nervous system, in part due to the ongoing nature of the traumas, and in part due to the fact that their primary caretakers—those the children rely on for stability, guidance, and protection—are the source of these traumas. Developmental traumas arise from ongoing neglect, abandonment, or abuse.

The impacts of chronic, relationally oriented trauma are pervasive and long lasting. All aspects of children's experiences become distorted. Their ability to self-regulate, experience relative control and mastery, think clearly, self-soothe, take care of themselves, recognize and articulate needs and feelings, feel worthy, focus attention, learn, trust others, bond, and stay physically healthy are all compromised, sometimes severely. Studies have shown that 75 percent of prison inmates suffer from developmental trauma.[2]

We vindicate our ancestors by transmuting their suffering
into a more enlightened way of being.

It is no surprise that the highly sensitive human heart is easily impacted by developmental trauma. Like the rest of the body and nervous system, the heart reacts to developmental trauma with the standard defensive repertoire of fighting, fleeing, or freezing. We lash out (fight) in our thinking, feeling, words, and behaviors at perceived aggressors; we avoid contact by physically distancing or inwardly withdrawing (flight); or we numb ourselves (freeze) so that we feel little or nothing. We also develop insecure attachment, or bonding, styles with others that continue throughout our adult lives unless we have a reparative relationship with a partner or a psychotherapist.

None of us had perfect parents, nor are we perfect ourselves. Reviewing our developmental history allows us to clearly see patterns of conditioning without judgment or blame. Although our parents and family members may have been the proximate agents of our obstructive conditioning, they were not the source of it. Psychological conditioning is handed down generation to generation, and we all consciously and unconsciously act it out. Certainly our parents and grandparents have had the most impact on us, yet humanity has a shared legacy of suffering that reaches back into prehistory. The more aware of it we are, the less we're likely to act on it.

We can break this ancient cycle of suffering, freeing ourselves and others from familial and cultural streams of conditioning by recognizing who we really are and by accepting and being with our conditioning in a spacious, intimate, and affectionate way. Doing so, we vindicate our ancestors by transmuting their suffering into a more enlightened way of being. Their suffering, for which we can feel compassion and understanding, is our wake-up call. In the end, we discover that psychological conditioning is not personal—it doesn't belong or refer to anyone. It is an unconscious heirloom of innocent confusion.

Cognitive insight into our reactive patterns is only a first step. This is why traditional talk therapy, particularly with an emotionally distant or poorly attuned therapist, is often ineffective. We also need to be able to sense our sensations, feel our feelings, recognize and question our core limiting beliefs, make sense of our experience, and rest in and as awareness.

Learning how to rest in and as awareness is the most important step. We need to be well-resourced when we delve into our psychological conditioning—loving, spacious awareness is our greatest resource. We can also significantly catalyze this process by entering into a trusting bond with another person—a sane family member, friend, partner, therapist, coach, or teacher.

Taking a Developmental Inventory

Take a few minutes to reflect in a nonjudgmental way on your own experience growing up. I invite you to take a break from reading this book right now and sit with the following questions. Take notes. Allow at least thirty minutes to answer this self-inventory, responding with more than a simple yes or no. You may want to take several sessions to do this. Sense your heart area as you respond, and pay close attention to your feelings.

> Did you feel mostly safe, seen, and loved in your family? If not, what did you experience?
>
> Were there patterns of neglect, abandonment, or abuse in your family?

Were you exposed to emotional or physical violence?

Were there losses of significant loved ones?
If so, how were they handled?

Did you often feel anxious, angry, depressed, or ashamed?

How did you adapt or defend yourself?

What impact did this conditioning have on your
ability to be in touch with your heart?

How has this conditioning affected your sense of self-worth?

How has this conditioning affected your relationships?

What have been the greatest resources for
your healing and sense of well-being?

What are you grateful for in your upbringing?

Take a minute to access the sense of spacious, loving awareness. Feel
it warmly embracing you and your conditioning just as you are. What
came up for you when answering the self-inventory above? Were there
any surprises? How does your heart area feel now? More importantly,
how are you with these experiences? Is there space for them to be as
they are?

Because the heart area is so emotionally and energetically sensitive and also such an accessible portal to our true nature, there is a
strong instinctive tendency to protect it when we are young. If we feel
attacked, abandoned, engulfed, or emotionally or physically neglected,
we shut down and armor ourselves. We numb and harden the heart
area, often unconsciously, distancing from our caretakers and ourselves.

There is also a cognitive dimension to our defense. We tell ourselves potent, distorted stories about our mistreatment and how we
must deal with it. Deep down we may believe that we deserve to be

abused or neglected, that something is wrong with us, or that we do not deserve to be loved, cared for, or protected. It can sometimes feel safer to blame ourselves than the caretakers we depend on. We may subconsciously conclude that we don't need anyone, that others are not safe to trust, and that we are alone in a hostile world. We may think that we are a misfit who has little worth or does not deserve to exist. We may believe that our life is a mistake.

What became frozen can thaw.
What hardened can soften.
What tensed can relax.

It is common to subconsciously conclude that we are fundamentally lacking or flawed. If our gaze turns inward, our heart may look or feel like a bombed-out crater or bottomless dark pit. It's certainly not a place we would want to visit or reveal to another person. This phenomenon of having an apparent hole in the heart area is common for those who have been neglected or abused. This is a form of *deficient emptiness*—a term coined by Hameed Ali, the founder of the Diamond Approach. Hameed, who goes by the pen name A. H. Almaas, distinguishes this kind of psychological emptiness from the full emptiness of our true nature that Julie described at the beginning of this chapter.[3] When we feel this sense of deficient psychological emptiness, we tend to avoid it and then act it out by looking to others to fill or distract us.

In addition to sexual attraction, this sense of fundamental lack is often a powerful element of romantic love. We project our unrecognized sense of intrinsic value onto others, hoping that they will recognize and restore us. This is due to what psychologists call a mirroring deficit.[4] Because our value was not accurately seen and mirrored back to us as children, we hope, mostly unconsciously, that our romantic partner will supply it. As a result, we strongly idealize our new partner and then quickly become disappointed in them. Sound familiar?

Since our sense of lack stems in part from poorly attuned or abusive parenting, it also becomes harder to find a suitable partner. We may not feel that we deserve loving attention, even as we crave it—we both want and fear clear, affectionate attention from another person. We will explore this critically important theme of relationship more fully in chapters 12 and 13.

Our hearts may feel numb, empty, or tightly contracted as a result of developmental trauma. The numbness is a defense against feeling lack or emotional pain. Intense feelings such as terror, shame, grief, and rage may have been too much to bear when we were young and felt so overwhelming and dysregulated. On a somatic level, we may have frozen or dissociated in response. Under great stress, we sometimes fragment. All of these strategies are designed to protect what is essential. One way or another, we bury our sensitivity, innocence, and openness.

However, there's excellent news: What became frozen can thaw. What hardened can soften. What tensed can relax. What became overly aroused can calm down. What was broken can mend. What was buried can be unearthed. What apparently died can resurrect. It takes time, patience, love, understanding, kindness, and often a little help from our friends (cue Ringo) for this to happen. As this healing and integration happens, perhaps slowly and never completely, we are increasingly grateful to simply be as we are.

Being with the Wounded Heart

In chapter 6, I described two approaches to being with our experience: stepping back and stepping into and through. Both approaches apply equally well to the heart. First, we don't need to go digging into the reactive conditioning stored in our heart—it's enough to just be with it whenever it arises. Digging tends to reinforce the ego's agenda for self-improvement, and in this work we accent remembering our native wholeness. You are whole regardless of your conditioning, and there is nothing fundamentally lacking or flawed about you. Let that in.

When you are aware of a disturbance in your heart area signaled by a somatic contraction or emotional reaction, allow it without judgment. Don't indulge the thought, *It shouldn't be here*, because this judgmental belief will only create distance. If the reaction is too strong to feel in the moment, take a step back and simply notice that you can sense and feel the reaction, noting that you are aware of it. Give your attention to this spacious awareness, even if it feels only like a sliver of space. Feel the edge of your reaction and what lies outside of it. Spacious presence is always here.

When you are ready, step from this sense of spacious presence into your experience with innocent, affectionate curiosity. Innocence means letting go of an agenda to get rid of or change your experience, which can prove challenging, particularly with uncomfortable feelings or sensations. Remember that when you are free of an agenda, you can be intimate with your experience.

Let yourself feel what you feel. Even numbness—the absence of feeling—is an experience. If there is sadness, let yourself feel sad. If there is shame, terror, guilt, doubt, rage, or anything else, just feel it without judgment. Breathe into it. If you are unfamiliar with feelings, take your time to recognize which feeling or combination of feelings you are experiencing. Once you are able to name the feeling, let it go. Feel it as pure sensation. How does it localize in your body? Does it have a form and density? What is in the center of it? This prior question can yield some surprising responses. Is there a belief that goes with this feeling and sensation? What is your deepest knowing about this belief?

The prior three paragraphs summarize my approach for guiding people to be with their experience as it arises. I sometimes joke that these are my trade secrets. I share them freely with you here and invite you to experiment with them as you'd like.

The Wounded Heart as a Portal

Wounds serve as excellent portals. This has been one of the most surprising discoveries I've made over my nearly forty years of in-depth exploration with people. Because the heart is the most easily accessible portal to our true nature, the wounds in the heart area are also potent paths to our essence. When we go all the way to the bottom of an apparently bottomless dark hole or frozen knot in our heart area, it opens into another dimension. Astonished and relieved, we discover what we have unknowingly protected all along—that which feels essential.

To illumine the sense of the separate–self
is to recognize its true nature
as the light of awareness.

When we feel that we have been abandoned by another person, particularly when we are children, we abandon ourselves. It's simply too painful and overwhelming to stay inwardly at home, so we leave—suddenly or gradually—according to the nature of our conditioning. The medicine for self-abandonment is affectionate, nonjudgmental attention directed to the depths of the heart area. Doing so, we reverse the movement of self-abandonment. We re-inhabit our self.

If in truth there is no localized Self, how can we speak of abandoning, recovering, or re-inhabiting our self? Isn't it enough to realize that the self is a fiction? In short, no. The longer and more nuanced answer is that, as humans, we are multidimensional, and it's important not to confuse the different levels. Infinite, nonlocalized awareness is having the localized experience of being an individual human that is you. Less formally stated, you are God in drag.

Although Being has no center or periphery, as human beings, we experience a relative sense of both. As we awaken to our true nature, this sense of having a center and periphery illumines and clarifies. These structures become more fluid and flexible. Some spiritual teachers and traditions refer to this as the clarified ego.

The point is to illumine the separate sense of self, not to annihilate it. To illumine the sense of the separate-self is to recognize its true nature as the light of awareness. Coming back to our core metaphor of the wave and the ocean of chapter 2, freedom and happiness do not come from flattening out a wave, but from knowing that the ocean is the source and substance of it. Besides, a completely flat ocean would be unnatural and rather boring!

When we are at home in our self, we feel and sense that we are really here, even though we cannot say exactly where *here* is. We inhabit our body fully even as we recognize that we are not limited to our body and that our body is not what we think it is. We feel the profound sensitivity of the heart area even as we know that we are not confined by the human heart. We are able to feel vibrantly, wakefully, and lovingly present. How do we accurately speak of this? The language of the self is tricky.

In 2009, the *New York Times Magazine* published a poignant article that described American Zen master Louis Nordstrom's experience in psychoanalysis. It's a classic story of so-called spiritual bypassing. Nordstrom had been physically abused by his mother, abandoned by both parents, and raised by alcoholic grandparents. Extremely bright, he excelled academically and had a precocious experience of no-self (kensho) as a beginning Zen student in the late 1960s. However, after receiving dharma transmission to teach in his lineage, leading meditation retreats, stumbling through multiple marriages, and scraping by financially with part-time academic positions, Nordstrom felt split within himself, both anxious and depressed. He also felt unseen—a self-described *invisible man*. Finally, in his sixties, he turned to a Buddhist-oriented therapist for help. After years of therapy, he gradually recognized his pattern of self-abandonment and allowed himself to grieve what he had lost. He writes:

> This abandoned life of mine is like the abandoned boy, and I am the mother I never had who returns to claim that life and embrace it. It is a source of great pathos to reflect that without the therapy experience I might have died without having been reunited with my life! And in that sense, without having truly lived.[5]

To truly live as a human being, we must embrace all aspects of our life. It's not enough to have profound glimpses of our true nature as no-self. We must, as Nordstrom did, face our life as it is and allow for the full range of our human experience, raw as it sometimes may be.

Essential Feelings

As we work our way through the various feelings associated with the heart area, their nature changes. They gradually become less reactive and egocentric. At first, they may feel highly personal. We may experience intense shame, unworthiness and self-loathing, a compelling fear of rejection, abandonment, attack, or engulfment, explosive rage, jealousy, envy, or sickening self-doubt. Terror and shame are often tightly interwoven and are usually the most common blocks to clearly sensing our inner knowing and acting in accord with it. I will sometimes ask my students or clients who are stuck at an apparent choice-point, "If you were free of fear and shame, how would you act?" A brief window of clarity often emerges for them, and the next obvious step will show itself, even if they are not quite ready to take it.

As we allow, feel, sense, tolerate, and come to understand these reactive feelings, they tend to lessen in both frequency and intensity. As we learn to neither suppress nor act them out, they gradually integrate, and we can receive their gifts—life energy is freed, clarity grows, the nervous system calms, the body relaxes, and the whole system is empowered. As this happens, essential feelings arise that are nonreactive, welling up from and through the Deep Heart: love, kindness, compassion, empathy, joy, delight, gratitude, appreciation, awe, wonder, and true humility.

As the Deep Heart awakens, these essential feelings become more easily accessible, almost as if a strong, clear spring has been unplugged. It feels natural to treat others with respect and kindness, and we naturally feel more empathy and compassion for our brothers and sisters, no matter their color, class, creed, age, size, sexual preference, or gender identity. Love arises naturally when we know that others are not essentially separate from us.

We feel grateful for no reason, simply happy to be alive. Life itself seems a miracle. A quiet, joyful contentment (*ananda*) radiates from the awakened heart. We feel genuinely humble and quietly confident. We trust that life will unfold as it needs to and that we are an empowered and creative participant in the unfolding.

We might still experience grief and anger, but they have a different quality. Grief feels like pure loss without an associated story of victimhood, of someone losing something essential, or of something that should not have happened. No-self righteous anger may occasionally arise to protect another life, like a mother bear protecting her cubs. When a genuine threat passes, however, the anger quickly subsides without leaving the typical residue of egoic resentment.

Buddhist mindfulness teachings encourage practitioners to cultivate heart-oriented essential feelings such as lovingkindness and gratitude. Whatever we put attention on grows, so there is value in consciously tending these qualities. For instance, it's helpful to briefly ask yourself what you feel grateful for before falling asleep or when you wake up.

The only potential drawback of such practices is that you may fall into self-judgment when old emotional patterns flare up, as they invariably do, and conclude that you are not being kind or grateful enough. You may also feel that you are not a good enough practitioner of mindfulness. However, if you remain patient with yourself and understand that failure is inevitable, this won't be a problem. It's also useful to know that these essential feelings are spontaneous byproducts of awakening to our true nature. As we grow in genuine self-recognition, kindness and gratitude quite naturally pour out from and through the depths of the heart.

~ Ten ~

IS IT SAFE TO SHINE?

Weapons cannot cut It, nor can fire burn It;
water cannot wet It, nor can wind dry It.
BHAGAVAD GITA, translated by T. N. Sethumadhavan

IN THIS CHAPTER I invite you to honestly explore two related questions: Does your heart still need to be protected as it once seemed to? Or is it safe now for you to open your heart and let it fully shine?

As much as we yearn to live from an open heart, we are often ambivalent about doing so. It's simultaneously what we most want and most fear. It's important to face our resistance and recognize that we are no longer children—we're aware adults who have capacities and resources we didn't possess when we were young.

Take some time to reflect on how open or defended your heart feels and whether it still needs protection. I'm not suggesting that you become naïve and utterly unguarded, but that you carefully examine the true nature of your heart from a present-time, mature, and illumined perspective.

The separate-inside-self—
that is, our story and image about our self—
always needs protection.
Our essential nature does not.

MEDITATIVE INQUIRY
What Is the True Nature
of Your Heart?

Find a quiet, comfortable place where you won't be interrupted for a few minutes, close your eyes, take a few deep breaths, and relax. As in earlier practices, be sure to give yourself ample time, pausing between each step.

1. Let your attention fall from your head into the heart area. Feel as if you can breathe directly into and out from the heart area.

2. Ask yourself: "What is the true nature of my heart?" Don't go to your mind for an answer. Let the question go. Be quiet. Listen, sense, and feel. There is no right response.

3. Let in what comes. Take as much time as you'd like.

4. When you are ready, ask yourself another question: "Does the true nature of my heart need protection?" Again, let the question work on you. Don't think about it.

5. Let in the response.

~

When I invite people to sit with these questions on retreat, the results are often revelatory in two ways. First, they discover, as perhaps you did, that their heart is intact, radiant, and full. Reports vary, of course, but people are uniformly surprised and delighted to discover a profound love, wisdom, warmth, openness, kindness, clarity, and gratitude in what feels like the core of their being, despite whatever beliefs they may have about themselves. Second, they realize that their heart of hearts, the very center of their being, does not need protection.

As one of my retreatants sat with these questions during an online session I led this morning, she reported experiencing a heartfelt image: "These arms of the infinite are holding me and everything in a loving embrace." She added, "I realize that I have always longed for this. The question about protection was meaningless."

The separate-inside-self—that is, our story and image about our self—always needs protection. Our essential nature does not. If there is only one experiential insight that you take away from reading this book, I hope it's that.

Knowing and feeling that our true nature cannot be hurt and therefore does not need to be protected is thoroughly liberating. This profound revelation counters all of our ordinary conditioning. How would your life change if you knew and felt without a doubt that you had nothing essential to protect? What would happen if you let yourself fully shine?

You would tell those you love that you love them.

You would speak the unarguable truth of your experience, without blame or judgment.

You would accept life as it is and respond creatively.

You would let yourself be moved by a fundamental current of love and wisdom.

You would be grateful to simply be.

You would openly cherish and support life.

You would share your gifts freely.

You would be a conscious vessel of kindness and clarity.

You would _____ (add your heart wisdom's upwelling here).

Something in our core knows all of this, and yet we become forgetful, confused, and fearful. The human heart does not exist in a vacuum. As a center of profound sensitivity and understanding, other aspects of our conditioning influence it. As I noted in earlier chapters, our mental clarity—our ability to see the limits of our ordinary, strategic thinking, as well as to see through our core limiting beliefs—allows our attention to drop into the heart. Similarly, our ability to feel safe in the world, particularly the world of people, is foundational for sustaining an openhearted way of being. If we don't feel safe, we won't open our heart—at least, not for long.

Under certain conditions, we may open our heart to people that we trust. We may even sometimes experience a generalized openheartedness toward life. This is common during the first blush of romantic love, but this particular kind of openheartedness is hard to sustain. If something triggers an underlying sense of danger, our heart shuts down and the inner light of being dims.

The human heart needs a foundation of safety to stay open. Just as a rose bush and its blossoms need the nourishment and support of the garden's earth, our emotional heart needs to feel a steady love and sense of safety as we grow up. As I've worked with people for decades, it's striking to see how primal the interconnection is between safety and openheartedness. If we feel unsafe with others because we have been physically or emotionally abandoned or attacked, it's extremely difficult to open our heart in a sustained way. On some level, we feel that few people, if any, can be trusted to a significant degree.

Emotionally and energetically, we learn to keep others at arms' length. One of my clients, Jared, calls this his Heisman approach, named after the straight-armed pose of the figure on the iconic trophy awarded to the best player in college football every year. Jared unconsciously adopted this stance after an early traumatic incident with his enraged and frightening father that was followed by a lack of protection from his mother. After this watershed event, Jared felt that real intimacy was too risky, that he could never completely let his guard down with others. This conclusion persisted on some level well into his adult life.

In an interesting synchronicity, a few days after I wrote that last paragraph, Jared and I had a session that helped to significantly illumine and relax his inner defensive stance and assist him in seeing that there is ultimately no one to defend. Afterward, he wrote the following account:

Early on in our session, I began to work with the trauma that I had been organized around since I was about seven years old. In particular, I was working with a part of me that I call *the Heisman*—my inner guard that almost never goes off duty.

As I was compassionately aware of this chronic inner defender, an image came up of a crack that went down the entire left side of my body—from my head, through my heart and gut, and all the way down to my foot. It also extended out in front of me, about as far away as my left hand could reach. It was like I was a giant cracked piece of wood, and the Heisman was protecting the crack.

I described this energetic and psychic crack, the ways that my body was patterned to maintain the crack, the Heisman, the shame and fear, the negative sense of self that was embedded in the crack, and the core belief that I was always vulnerable to being violated. John received it all with love, respect, and lucidity.

Then I began to ask whether or not I'm safe *now*. I silently checked in with John, his office, my inner adult, my inner child, and my true Self to see if it was safe, and the answer was—on deeper and deeper levels—yes. This line of questioning evolved, and I started wondering whether or not I even had a self that needed guarding. The answer was—again, on deeper and deeper levels—no. It became clear that I was not actually who I thought I was. I was vast, in union with everyone and everything, and made of light. As this dawned on me, I increasingly shined.

From this state of clarity, I studied the crack and realized that it didn't ultimately exist. The Heisman became obsolete and fell away. I considered what I should do next with my massive self-healing project, and I became curious if I needed a project at all. I discovered that I didn't. After all, there was no one that needed fixing. I entered into a totally relaxed space and started "going with the flow" to an extraordinarily unfamiliar extent. My most deeply held knot began quickly working itself out. I was amazed and made a remark about how much gets done when we're not trying.

As Jared faced and intimately embraced the knot of his core psychological wound, a spontaneous inquiry arose that unveiled his native wholeness—what he sometimes calls his Buddha nature. Then, as he felt increasingly relaxed and radiant, his chronic defensive stance fell away, and the knot of conditioning began to work itself out without any conscious effort.

Once Jared described his core wound with such graphic and precise imagery—a crack running all the way down his left side, including his heart area—it was fascinating to observe how a spontaneous movement of inquiry arose in the form of these two essential questions: (1) Was he safe now? and (2) Was there anyone to defend? These quickly unlocked two related insights. As he was able to acknowledge that he was outwardly and inwardly safe, it also quickly became clear that there was not an inside-separate-self to defend. Jared intimately knew, felt, and sensed that his true nature was vast, luminous, and undivided. His "wave-tip self" recognized its oceanic nature, and it was completely obvious that the ocean did not need a defender. This realization created an optimal environment for his rigid defense to relax and for this wound to heal. A small miracle had unfolded on its own. Was he safe now? Yes! Was there a self to defend? No! Jared's knot didn't fully release after this dramatic session, but another important step unfolded in his self-understanding, self-acceptance, and transformative process.

*All of us are infinitely bigger than the little britches
of our core limiting beliefs.*

After attending several of my retreats, Glenn—who is a long-time student of inner work—met with me individually to explore the depths of his heart. After his first session, he wrote:

> I found myself wanting to become more intimate with the heart. [When I looked inside] it had a golden tint to it . . . a condensed richness whose affect was a love of the purest kind. I saw that what I truly love *is* this love.
>
> [This process] is a surrendering open, dropping a defense to love. If I can give in, the defensive holding—often in the chest somewhere—gives way and morphs into this golden love.
>
> The deeper presence of this pure love brings into clearer relief a surface layer that covers it. Simply being with this layer reveals what it is about. In my case, it has to do with survival, holding myself up, basic trust, and a (negative) transference onto male authority figures.
>
> Even though these ostensibly obstructing layers over the deeper Love-Heart are there, I can still feel that Love-Heart underneath. Recognizing this amplifies the heart's presence, which in turn exerts a quiet influence on the defensive structures, bringing them more fully into conscious awareness to be felt, seen, and released.

After his session Glenn noted:

> For two people to have the opportunity to do this work in the world is revolutionary. It's so easy to be lost in the world's lost-ness. This True Heart is the basis of sanity. Without it, humanity is lost.

This simple observation rings true for me—the Awakened Heart is the basis of true sanity. With his inner vision, Glenn could see and feel a pure gold light of love in the depths of his heart. He also recognized that it was this love that he most loved. As he directly experienced this underlying gold-suffused *Love-Heart*, the defensive layers that covered it became more conscious. They also began to transform, gradually morphing into love. As part of this process, he could see the origins of those layers in his fear of survival. This primal fear led him to distrust himself and life, to armor himself by contracting inwardly and tightly holding himself up, and to fear male authority figures. The impacts were pervasive. Glenn's overall coping strategy was to stay small and hidden. Can you relate?

In one form or another, far too many of us have learned this lesson to stay small. As a child, were you ever told that you were too big for your britches? There's an unintended kernel of truth in this shaming statement. In fact, all of us are infinitely bigger than the little britches of our core limiting beliefs. Similarly, the voice that belittles us (for example, "Who do you think you are?") can transmute into genuine self-inquiry when it relinquishes the harsh attitude of the inner critic. Who *do* I actually think I am? It's fun to use a bit of mental aikido to turn our judging mind toward discernment. In this way, inner accusations can easily transmute into heartfelt insights and inquiries.

In our second session, Glenn tapped into a fundamental life current and felt held, supported, and moved by something greater than his ordinary self. He wanted to trust this current and its accompanying sense of power, but he noticed a resistance to doing so that came with anger and bitterness. As he explored these feelings, he became aware of a belief and a feeling that it was unsafe to trust life or to express his inner clarity. As a child, doing so had led to confrontations with and attacks from his father.

When Glenn again sensed into his clarity and the power that came with it in present time, he felt a distinctive radiance in the heart area. He could imagine saying to his father and others, "I disagree. I see it differently. That's not true for me." Glenn saw the old defensive network illumined from the inside and realized that when he had been trusting as a boy, he had felt tricked and betrayed by life. As he attuned with a deeper current of life in the present moment, Glenn saw that a discerning trust was possible that was different from the naïve trust of his childhood. Now he could trust with clear eyes. It was an empowering and heartening realization—it was now actually safe to shine.

~ *Eleven* ~

WHAT ABOUT THE GUT,
OR HARA?

A human being has so many skins inside,
covering the depths of the heart . . .
Go into your own ground and learn to know yourself there.
MEISTER ECKHART

WHENEVER I TEACH about heart wisdom, someone will inevitably ask, "What about the gut?" Great question! The heart and the gut are, not surprisingly, intimately interrelated. An illumined gut supports the heart, and an Awakened Heart illumines the gut. As humans, we need to feel safe in order to keep our heart open, and our gut is directly involved with a foundational sense of safety (and, as we shall see, quite a bit more).

By gut, I'm referring to the belly, also known as the *hara* in Japanese. This part of the physical body ranges from the solar plexus to the tailbone, and we can sense its center a few finger widths below the navel in the interior of the body. In Taoism, this location is known as the *dan tien* ("elixir field" or "sea of qi"). As it awakens, we feel the hara as a radiant disc of warmth encompassing the entire belly. Energetically, it includes the lower three energy centers, or chakras.

The more we attune with reality, the more grounded we feel.

The essential quality of the hara is stability—the sense of being fundamentally grounded, but also spacious at the same time. As the hara awakens, people describe a sense of the ground that feels increasingly open and expansive. This spacious, open quality is difficult to describe—it's a paradox for the ordinary mind, but we can palpably sense it. Some contemplative traditions formulate this subtle sense as an ultimate groundlessness while others describe it as a groundless ground.

We resolve the apparent paradox of spacious ground when we realize that reality is inherently grounding. The more we attune with reality, the more grounded we feel. For example, once we know the facts of a given situation—the status of our health or the state of our relationship with someone—we're able to deal with it a lot more realistically, even if we're initially disoriented by the new information. If our body is sick or our relationship needs more attention, acknowledging the facts allows us to deal with the situation more consciously and effectively. Even if it's difficult to do so at first, something within us relaxes as we face reality, and we come into greater congruence with our inner knowing as well as with the facts on the ground. I invite you to reflect on this in the following short practice.

MEDITATIVE INQUIRY
Facing Reality and the Experience of Grounding

Reflect on a time when you had to face a difficult truth in your life. How grounded did you feel before you directly faced it? How did the situation resolve? Did you feel less or more grounded as a result?

~

The inherently grounding nature of reality applies equally well to the discovery of who we really are. Ordinarily, we subconsciously cling to a story of being a flawed, limited, and separate self. In truth, our highly conditioned, normal identity is not who we really are, but we become ungrounded when we believe in this identity. We have a nagging sense of being a fraud, of not being fully real, and something in us knows that we are living a lie. We also feel an underlying subtle anxiety.

By consciously and subconsciously taking a stand as an illusory separate-self, we rely on a false ground, clinging to it for dear life. On some level, we feel like a little polar bear on a melting chunk of arctic ice, doubting that we can swim.

When our provisional ground feels threatened, as it often does, we tend to grasp it more tightly. Questioning and letting go of our familiar story is disorienting, sometimes greatly so—it can feel as if our ground is falling away or being pulled out from under us like a rug. Understandably, we resist losing our known foothold. For this reason, self-honesty and vulnerability are critically important qualities on this path. Do we really want to know the truth? Are we willing to give up our most cherished illusions for it? Most of us are reluctant to let go of our familiar identities because we imagine that they keep us safe.

What happens if we lose our chronic grip? The conditioned mind fears a free fall into a terrifying abyss and reflexively projects and resists an imaginary annihilation. The reality is quite different. When we truly relax and let go, our familiar contracted ground softens and melts, and we have the sense of tapping into the source of life itself—a luminous darkness full of pure potentiality unfolds in our awareness. We begin to sense an underground ballast like the keel of a sailboat, and we feel supported by an invisible, unshakeable, and unchanging ground. As a result, we are less likely to "keel over" when challenging circumstances arise. Instead, we sense a fathomless resilience.

MEDITATION
Opening to the Ground

Find a place where you won't be disturbed, sit comfortably upright, close your eyes, and take several deep, slow breaths.

Feel the weight of your body held by whatever you are sitting on. Then relax into being held.

Bring your attention to your pelvis and imagine that you can directly inhale from and exhale into the ground beneath your feet.

Let your exhalation completely empty out into a bottomless space beneath your body.

Wait for the inhalation to come of its own, as if it is also arising from the space below.

Allow your attention to completely dissolve into this bottomless, open space.

Be this space and rest in it for as long as you like.

~

Survival, Sex, and Power: An Overview

Because the hara encompasses the lower energy centers, it governs the primal instinctual drives for survival, sex, and interpersonal power, the latter of which is used to establish social hierarchy. It also includes the compelling and sometimes overwhelming emotions of terror, lust, rage, and shame. It's a denser, less conscious, more instinctual domain. No wonder that most spiritual traditions—both Eastern and Western—judge it, downplay its significance, or avoid it entirely. We do so at tremendous cost.

This devaluation creates an inner split. Spiritual teachings tend to focus on illuminating the body from the heart area up, leaving the nether lands of the guts in the dark. As a result, some spiritual practitioners report feeling cut off at the midline of their body. I recently led an online retreat entitled "Awakening the Head, Heart, and Hara" and found that the hara was unknown territory to many of the participants, some who were decades-long veterans of the spiritual quest.

It's like this for many of us—the hara is a key missing piece. Without it, we can easily feel ungrounded, subtly dissociated, and not fully here. We do not inhabit the core of our body nor do we fully trust our inner authority. If we split ourselves in this way, we are unable to be truly autonomous—that is, stand on our own two feet or take our seat in our inner knowing. Our spiritual understanding can feel as if it pertains to another, more ethereal realm—irrelevant and unwelcomed in this dense, earthly domain.

At some point we will need to come out
of our metaphoric cave or monastery
and face the reality of our human life.

I felt this split within myself during my early and midtwenties. I practiced and briefly taught the aptly named Transcendental Meditation. I was seeking a transcendent freedom—a way to rise up and out of my experience as an anxious human being—and in fact I was resisting being here as I am and opening to life as it is. As a result, I became energetically top-heavy, developing the subtle mind but feeling less grounded and vital. After multiple months-long meditation courses, I was often sick, exhausted, and spacey.

If we exclude the hara, our spiritual quest can become arid and lifeless. When we are out of touch with our instinctual energies, we tend to get sick more often and also have difficulty setting interpersonal boundaries with others. Further, we may be ambushed on occasion by reactive feelings because if we merely step away from them into spacious presence, they will continue to trigger us from time to time. Our unwelcome guests clamor at the door, no matter how many times we ignore them and push them away. This happens because we're side-stepping something important—namely, our vitality and grounded stability.

This subtle, complex, and vitally important domain of human experience cannot be divorced from the quest for spiritual awakening, not if we want awakening to be embodied and relevant to daily life. A renunciate approach will not work—at least, not for long, and certainly not if we want to actively engage in the world. At some point we will need to come out of our metaphoric cave or monastery and face the reality of our human life, as difficult and gritty as it sometimes is.

The hara is associated with several profound existential themes: overidentification with the body, attachment to desire, and the illusion of personal agency. Each of us must face and see through these compelling issues during our journey of self-recognition. Given the importance of the subject, the awakening of the hara and discovery of our deepest ground deserves a book of its own. I'll only touch briefly on some of the key themes here.

Our most basic identification is with our physical body. When we think about our self, we are usually referring to the body that we imagine we inhabit, and this identification is so ingrained and consensually validated that we rarely question it. As an esoteric aside, a few of my clients and students report remembering the moment when they arrived in their body as an infant in the womb, usually with the brakes fully on! They report feeling as if they were being forced to enter a tiny, miserable prison cell. I've heard Adyashanti describe a primal shock that happens when consciousness identifies with a specific body, with or without resistance to incarnating.

This largely unconscious process of identification starts from the bottom up—that is, from the base of the spine to the top of the head. This process progresses through an overlapping spectrum of instinctual, emotional, and mental realms of experience that corresponds with the chakra system with its lower to higher vibrational levels and with the evolutionary development of the physical brain: the brainstem (the reptilian brain, which connects with the amygdala-driven survival reactions located in the limbic system), the limbic system (the mammalian brain and emotions), and the neocortex (primates and their developed cognitive abilities). The main point is that we are hardwired to survive as biological organisms and are therefore fundamentally identified with our physical body.

If unconscious identification is a bottom-up process, spiritual awakening is generally top-down. It makes sense. Wakeful awareness tends to first illumine thought, then feelings, and finally more instinctual domains in the process of waking down. I am presenting this unfolding awakening of the body as if it proceeds in a linear descending order, but this isn't how it happens. The actual process of awakening and transformation has a number of twists and turns that opens in a unique fashion and timetable for everyone.

It's generally easier to disidentify from our thoughts than it is from our body because it feels as if a lot more is at stake with our body. It's usually easier to see that our thoughts do not define us, even if we sometimes become identified with particular belief systems and in extreme instances even sacrifice our life on their behalf, as in the case of political and religious ideologues of all stripes.

Our feelings are more compelling and less conscious than our thoughts. As a result, they tend to be even stickier. Have you noticed how hard it is to think straight or listen when you are experiencing an overwhelming feeling? Furthermore, we're often convinced that if we feel something strongly that it must be true, especially if we have a more emotional nature.

Our instinctual identifications are even less conscious and more embedded than our thinking and feeling. For example, when our biological survival feels threatened, our nervous system becomes hyperaroused and dysregulated, inducing overpowering fight-flight-freeze reactions. We go on automatic. Terror trumps everything else.

In my long-term, in-depth work with clients, the terror of annihilation is usually the final layer of conditioning they flush out and work through. It takes a lot of resources, inner and outer, to face this domain of experience, especially if we have been exposed to developmental trauma. This level of conditioning is so opaque that its illumination requires great patience, understanding, and self-acceptance. Fortunately, this final layer can gradually transform over time.

Survival

In chapter 3 of *In Touch*, I discuss the various themes associated with the root survival chakra. I'll briefly summarize them here, but I first want to say a few words about the role of the chakras.

You may tend to discount the existence of these subtle energy centers if you have not directly experienced them yourself. That's understandable, but the chakras are quite real and particularly relevant to the process of embodying your true nature in everyday life, whether or not you ever consciously experience them.

These subtle energy centers are impacted by our conditioning. When they contract, they influence the way that we sense, feel, think, and act. For instance, when the root chakra is contracted, we feel ungrounded as well as cut off from the flow of primal life energy. As we work through these contractions, we may sense the emergence of a spacious energy body and feel ourselves as translucent vehicles for the light of awareness. It's a true delight to witness how friends, students, and clients literally light up as they free themselves from the veils of conditioning and more clearly recognize their true nature.

At a recent day-long retreat, a spirited eighty-five-year-old nun asked about the nature of love and the experience of the bodily incarnation of spirit. As I described how our subjective sense of the body changes with awakening—becoming more fluid, spacious, and illumined—she began to glow.

"You are lighting up," I said.

"What do you mean?" she asked.

"Check inside," I replied. "Do you feel lighter?"

"Yes, I do!" she said with some surprise.

"Something in you is recognizing what I am describing,"
I added, as a beautiful smile lit her aging face.

The root chakra—which we can detect at the very base of the spine—is directly involved with our sense of safety and survival. If we feel chronically unsafe in the world, this energy center will be contracted. Our psychological sense of self is intimately tied to our physical body. Accordingly, when our self-image feels threatened, it often feels as if our physical existence is also at risk, which is one reason that the process of spiritual awakening can feel so threatening for some people—opening up can look and feel like annihilation. We project our most unconscious fears onto the unknown.

Thus, if we have experienced some early rupture or distortion in bonding with our primary caretaker—usually our mother—we live in terror of abandonment or engulfment on some level. The feeling is much stronger than ordinary fear. People who know terror firsthand will immediately resonate with this more dramatic description.

Further, the earlier and deeper the rupture is, the less of a story we have about it. Narratives about our unworthiness, how others can't be trusted, and how unsafe the world is come later and reinforce an unconscious predisposition. Conditioned imprints in these cases are not just stories—they are powerfully embedded in the nervous system and the body. Our unconscious reactions are somatic and visceral, prior to any thought.

As a result, it's not enough to solely question the truth of a story in order to clear this kind of conditioning. Cognitive approaches, no matter how refined or spiritually infused, have limited impact. We will also need to sense and feel into our body in a carefully paced and well-resourced way, often within the context of a relationship that feels both safe and attuned. Professional help can be a valuable resource and catalyst, and the process takes time and can't be forced. Patience and self-acceptance are important.

A large number of us have not been exposed to developmental trauma and feel relatively safe in the world. Even if we've been fortunate in this way, we still tend to strongly identify with our body. However, as we progress in our spiritual quest, our sense of body identification and ground will subtly shift, and another paradox emerges: As we inhabit our body more intimately, we will feel less bound by it. We will eventually discover that the very center of the body—a transparent, vibrant, and illumined core—feels one with the whole of life.[1]

Our sense of the body changes, becoming more spacious, fluid, lively, and open. We feel ourselves grounded and present and, at the same time, less localized. This isn't a dissociative reaction. There is no aversive relationship to the body. Instead, a multidimensional sense of the ground naturally emerges, and we increasingly feel in the world and not of it—but not in a mentally induced, detached way. We actually feel *more* intimate with our body and the apparent external world. We realize that we *are* this body, and so much more. After initially disidentifying from an *exclusive* identification with the body, we include it within an expansive version that embraces the whole of life. Nothing is excluded; everything is included. This is the real meaning of Tantra—increasingly we experience that the ordinary is sacred.

> *When we bring sex out of the shadows*
> *and into the light of awareness,*
> *it tends to slow down, lighten up,*
> *and become more connected to our heart,*
> *body, and the whole of life.*

Sex

Sex is a hot topic—spiritual teachers and students trip over it all the time. It's far too common for teachers (typically male) to exploit their students for sexual favors and then rationalize the violation as a special gift or teaching. Thankfully, more people (mostly women) are stepping forward to honestly report these damaging experiences.

Why does this happen in the first place? I suspect several factors are at play, one of which I've already mentioned: the lower half of the body is generally excluded or devalued by most spiritual traditions. As a result, sexuality remains in the shadows and is unconsciously acted out. Another reason lies in the fact that the vast majority of religions are traditional, male-dominated hierarchies, which—when confronted with the reality of sexual abuse—tend to react by focusing on doing whatever it takes to protect the brotherhood. The same tendency holds true for cults that center around a charismatic male leader. Fortunately, there are many wonderful male and female spiritual teachers who don't act out sexually and who help their students, congregations, and sanghas.

When we bring sex out of the shadows and into the light of awareness, it tends to slow down, lighten up, and become more connected to our heart, body, and the whole of life. As we become more intimate with our true nature in an increasingly embodied way, we naturally feel more inwardly fulfilled. Our core lights up. We continue to enjoy life, often taking joy in the most ordinary experiences, even as we come to understand that our happiness does not depend upon any circumstance. Knowing that wealth, power, social status, and sexual experiences will not make us happy allows us to relate to these conditions and energies much more lightly.

But we have seen that spiritual awakening by itself is often not sufficient—it also requires self-honesty. The love for authenticity and transparency fuels a willingness to directly face our own incongruencies along with the denial and rationalizations that accompany them. This takes humility. It also takes courage to ask your deepest knowing the following questions:

What am I unwilling to see about myself?

What am I avoiding?

Take a moment to try it out now. Feel and see what comes up. The truth eventually frees us, bringing greater inner ease and harmony.

As we awaken and mature, our relationship to sexuality changes. We become less interested in the goal of orgasm or sexual conquest and more engaged in the process of sharing in an intimate way. We take our time and are able to stop at any moment. We attune with feelings of love and appreciation and also tap into a larger life current, of which *eros* is but one stream. Within the context of open awareness, sexuality gradually transmutes into a beautiful, conscious celebratory path of shared dissolution into wholeness. It increasingly changes into true moment-to-moment lovemaking. Jean Klein described it this way:

In supreme intimacy, there is sensitivity and a great sense of beauty and elegance. Body relationship is a crowning physical manifestation of the togetherness of a spiritual state. But for the body relation to be elevated to such heights, it must come as a spontaneous outflowing between two lovers living really in oneness.[2]

Sexual pleasure is only one form of sensuality. Even if we are not sexually active or particularly interested in sex, our sensuality naturally expands and finds expression through other channels. All of the senses become more receptive (a process Jean Klein described as the "restoration of the senses").[3] The way that we see, hear, touch, taste, and smell opens up because we are more present to our actual experience, which feels increasingly fresh and new. Perception is more direct, less mediated by thought, and freer of any grasping. Our internal running commentary—typically filled with judgments and comparisons of ourselves and others—quiets down. We are more available to sense the beauty that is here—a simple birdsong, an autumn leaf on the sidewalk, and the aging lines in our mirrored face, sculpted by laughter and tears.

If your attention has become fixated on sex in an obsessive way, be curious, attentive, and nonjudgmental. First, be a witness to the process and carefully note all the shifts of attention—the stories that the mind tells in justification or in fantasy, feelings, and intense bodily sensations before, during, and after having sex. Notice that there is awareness throughout the experience and then experiment with briefly postponing the impulse to sexually act. Wait five minutes and notice what happens. You'll often find that the wave of desire rises and falls, and you might experience a kind of burn. Be with it. Tolerate it. Notice how you feel after doing so. Wait ten minutes the next time around, and so on. When the fever diminishes a bit, accent the sense of presence—spacious, loving awareness—and attune with it for a few minutes. Then allow both the light of awareness and sexual desire and sensation to coexist simultaneously. What happens when you do so? As with other forms of conditioning, a spontaneous integrative process will unfold over time.

For some people, sexuality is a particularly intense form of desire. For others, desire constellates around food, alcohol, drugs, money, shopping, or work, stimulating the release of dopamine—the brain's pleasure and reward system.[4] Each fixation offers an opportunity to explore what it is that we most desire. All relative desires lead back to our most primal desire—to knowingly be who we are and to live this understanding in our daily life. Suppressing desire doesn't work, not for long, but consciously exploring the very core of desire does. All experiences are portals to our true nature.

Control and Interpersonal Power: From Willfulness to Willingness

The upper range of the hara includes the solar plexus, which governs issues of control and interpersonal power and is also directly linked to the survival issues that localize at the base of the spine. These two centers closely coordinate. Most people can more easily sense a contraction in the area of the solar plexus than in the pelvic bowl. If you are operating out of some residual terror, you will usually sense it first in the solar plexus—it feels like a clenched fist or tight knot.

This is the area where I have historically held the most tension. As a sensitive boy, I learned to avoid the occasional hard look in my mother's eyes and cold tone of her voice by overcontrolling my emotions and actions. This took the form of holding my breath (which created diaphragmatic tension) and subtly clenching my solar plexus to brace against potential disapproval. Forty years ago, a psychic told me that it looked like I had a steel manhole cover over my solar plexus—a disturbingly accurate read. Fortunately, it has softened over the years.

What are we trying to control? Everything! Ourselves, others, and the world. Interpersonal power dynamics center in this area. We subconsciously scan others' faces for emotions, listen to their voice tones, observe their physical postures, and try to decode the real meaning of their verbal messages in order to find out whether they approve of us, whether we fit in, and what our status is. Social hierarchy runs throughout the animal kingdom; humans are no exception. It's ingrained in our cultural history, particularly since the agrarian revolution when social stratification intensified. Our nomadic hunter-gatherer ancestors were much more egalitarian, peaceful, and healthy before they settled down to domesticate plants and animals around twelve thousand years ago.[5]

We are more attuned with what is needed
and less attached to doing something perfectly
or achieving a particular outcome.

We try to be in control in order to survive. Our ordinary mind, with its super powers to decode patterns and imagine possibilities, is implicated in the process. We think that if we can *know*, we can *control*, which means we can *survive*. As you might guess, most of this operates below our conscious awareness.

Unfortunately, when our impulse to control is not tempered with the heart, we try to dominate others. We see this during the *terrible twos* when children discover their personal will, in family systems in which one parent terrorizes and controls their spouse and children, and with authoritarian leaders who abuse their power. Dramatic power struggles such as these populate several of Shakespeare's tragedies. It's an ancient human story.

This center of the personal will relates to our sense of agency, defined here as "the feeling of control over actions and their consequences."[6] This is called the sense of *doership* in Vedanta, as in, "I am the doer." But are we really? Do we initiate, execute, and control our actions? It certainly seems like it, but recent brain research shows that the actions we assume we are choosing begin in the brain milliseconds or even seconds before the mind consciously decides to choose them.[7] In other words, conscious choice may only be an afterthought!

As the apparently separate *I* discovers its true nature, the sense of personal agency changes. Increasingly, we feel that while doing is happening, no one is doing. Choices are made, but no one is choosing. In fact, the more clearly we recognize this, the more fitting, functional, and on the mark our choices become. We feel freer, more spontaneous, more trusting, and at the same time less impulsive. Rather than either forcing our way or collapsing into helplessness, we become more responsive to the whole situation. We are more attuned with what is needed and less attached to doing something perfectly or achieving a particular outcome.

Quality continues to be important, but the creative process takes precedence over the final product. We sense a natural flow of intelligence and trust that things will work out as they need to. As we increasingly see through the illusion of being in total control, a more profound sense of letting go unfolds, and we gradually trust that something vaster than the limited mind is running the show.

In religious terms, *my* will surrenders to *thy* will, although it is not as dualistic as such language would suggest. It's more as if a wave senses its oceanic nature and attunes to the stillness and subtle currents that are present in its depths. The apparently personal will aligns more intimately with something (which, again, is not a thing) more fundamental than the ordinary mind. Roberto Assagioli, who along with Carl Jung was an early pioneer of transpersonal psychology, called this the transpersonal will.[8] We become truly open and responsive. *Willfulness* gradually transmutes into an alert, nonpassive *willingness*.

This willingness applies to all of our experiences, whether we think of them as outer or inner. We get out of the business of manipulating our self and others. On a practical level, this means that we accept our experience as it is—instead of asking, "What *should* I be experiencing?" we ask, "What *am* I experiencing?" and become—in the words of existential psychologist James Bugental—*experience near*.[9] We experience this in its purest form during silent meditation when we rest in and as awareness without trying to change our experience in any way, but we can also sense this in our active daily life.

Allowing our experience is not the same as unconsciously acting it out. Instead, we carefully observe our experience as it is, allowing ourselves to feel what we feel and sense what we sense. For example, if we feel anger radiating from our solar plexus, we let ourselves fully experience it without being compelled to express it to another person. The same holds true for anxiety, shame, or any corresponding knot of tension. If we do express our feelings, we do so in a cleaner and more conscious manner, freer of blame and projection. We realize that no one *makes us* feel as we do. We do that to ourselves, no matter what the external trigger may be.

As we get out of the business of manipulating our own experience and become more willing to experience whatever is happening here in this body-mind, we naturally get out of others' business. Our attempts to control and manipulate other people stems directly from our own lack of self-acceptance and self-knowledge. The more open we are to our self as we are, the more space we give to others—we no longer believe that they need to change in order for us to be happy. Relationships become more simple, peaceful, and loving.

Of course, self-regulation requires some degree of functional control. The point here is to let go of unneeded control, the type that constrains inspiration and creative movement. As we surrender to our deepest knowing, spontaneous inclinations to do or not do, or to do in a certain way, naturally arise with more clarity, and our life becomes a creative process—more like a living work of art.

MEDITATION
Attuning with the Hara

As with prior meditations, allow at least a minute between each of the following steps.

1. Find a quiet, comfortable place where you won't be interrupted for the next few minutes.

2. Close your eyes, take a few deep breaths, and relax.

3. Remind yourself that there is no problem to solve right now and that it is all right to not know.

4. Notice that the weight of your body is held by the chair or whatever you are sitting upon. Let yourself be held.

5. Allow your attention to drop down from the head to your lower belly and imagine that you can directly inhale and exhale from this area. As a sensate reminder, you can also place your hands here.

6. Sense into the interior of your lower belly as you breathe, opening to whatever you experience. Without effort, simply notice if this center opens or changes in any way.

7. Continue this lightly held focus for another ten minutes. If your mind wanders, bring attention back to the hara.

8. If you fall into a deep silence, let go of any focusing and simply rest in and as this vibrant silence for as long as you like.

~

~ Twelve ~

THE HEART IN RELATIONSHIP I

Love, Lack, and Fullness

When you know beyond all doubting
that the same life flows through all that is,
and you are that life, then you will love
all naturally and spontaneously.
NISARGADATTA MAHARAJ, *I Am That*

NISARGADATTA—the loquacious, luminous-eyed, bidi-smoking sage from Mumbai, India—gets right to the heart of the matter: Love spontaneously arises from knowing that the same life flows through all and we are that life. How well do you know this firsthand? At first-heart?

This revelation is so profound that we can barely speak of it. Yet we can intimately know and feel this open secret as surely as we feel the warmth of the sun as the fog clears. To relate from and as the Great Heart—from and as our essential nature—is to be in communion with the totality of life. But even the word *communion* is subtly misleading. It's not as if two come together and become one—it's more that we see and feel through an apparent division. The seer and the seen—the lover and the Beloved—were never two.

When we relate primarily from the Great or Universal Heart, we experience life as Nisargadatta describes it and feel a natural outpouring of love and gratitude for no reason. We meet others as expressions of our essential nature and are open to them as they are. Jean Klein notes, "In this communion, the so-called other's presence is felt as a spontaneous giving and our own presence is a spontaneous receiving."[1]

This essential receptivity, free of self-image and story, welcomes life as it is. We receive others as the gifts that they are. We also have the visceral sense that we are meeting our deepest self disguised in another form. The light of awareness shines through and as wildly variable physical forms and points of view, and we experience a special delight to consciously share this understanding with another. This often happens spontaneously during meditative gazing or with friends who share this path of self-recognition. As conventional division dissolves, people wonder if they are seeing themselves or the other person. It baffles the ordinary mind: Is it *me* or *you* that I am seeing? Yes, it is.

This way of being with others is utterly uncontrived. We are not trying to be positive, to see the good in others, or to be loving. We are not trying to be mindful in our relationships, as useful as that effort may sometimes be. Instead, this open receptivity is a natural byproduct of self-recognition. When we no longer take our self as a separate someone, we are free to truly meet others. Even if we are not drawn to spend time with some people, or need to set clear boundaries with others, we still intuit their true nature and know that they are not essentially separate from us. We can inwardly bless them and truly wish them well.

Perhaps you have glimpsed this essential way of meeting. Can you recall a time when you unconditionally loved another person? Parents often experience this with their children. Many of us have also felt this when we fell in love with someone special or discovered an abiding love for our partners, friends, or family members. I invite you to take a few minutes to attune with this quality of meeting. Again, be sure to allow for pauses, and don't go to your mind for an answer as you explore the following inquiry. Take as much time as you need.

MEDITATIVE INQUIRY
Unconditional Love

Sit quietly, close your eyes, and take a few deep breaths.

Bring your attention to the heart area in the center of your chest and imagine that you can inhale and exhale directly from this area.

Think of someone in your life for whom you feel or felt unconditional love. Focus your attention on the feeling of love and let go of the image of the person.

Notice the subtle sensations in the heart area. Let your attention go deeply into the core of these sensations and feelings.

Is there a center or boundary to this love?

Is it possible that you share this openhearted love with all beings?

Is it possible that this loving awareness is who you, everyone, and everything really is?

~

This natural openheartedness is never far away, but it is regularly obscured by the limiting beliefs and feelings that we hold about our self and others. Relationships bring these obscurations out in spades. It's where we get most triggered. But while these reactions are emotionally painful and disturbing, they are also opportunities for clarity. I encourage you to think of them as part of your advanced studies—one of the more challenging assignments of the human curriculum!

If we want to make a real difference,
we need to be able to step out
of the cycle of reactivity.

It is important that our spiritual awakening yields more than a sense of inner freedom; it also needs to radiate out into all of our relationships. For this to happen, our heart must also awaken. It's not enough to be an enlightened misanthrope—that is, someone who knows his or her true nature on the level of the mind but who remains unkind and unloving to others. When awakening does not touch our heart and relationships, it remains immature.

This is true whether we are talking about friends, families, communities, or nations. Brian Victoria provides a sobering assessment of how easily Zen teachers and teachings were seduced and used by Japanese militarists before and during the second world war (Suzuki Roshi, who lived in Japan at the time and later founded San Francisco Zen Center, was a notable exception).[2] The nature and extent of our spiritual awakening also impacts the biosphere and our fellow living creatures. How are we moved to act as our mind, heart, and body open? The answer will vary for each of us. Few of us will be called to act on the world stage like a Dalai Lama, Nelson Mandela, or Gandhi, but all of us can practice both the intentional and spontaneous acts of kindness, clarity, gratitude, and generosity that will help turn the tide of ignorance and suffering. More than ever, we need everyone's contribution, especially in the field of relationships. At the very least, we can begin by listening more carefully to one another and responding with more honesty and compassion.

If we want to make a real difference, we need to be able to step out of the cycle of reactivity. This means that we need to clearly see our triggers and diffuse them as they arise. This is an ongoing process—perfection is not the goal. It's enough that we consciously engage in the process of clearing our mind, opening our heart, illumining our gut, and acting from our deepest knowing. We need to be willing to intimately be with our experience as it is. All relationships with others start with our relationship with our self.

As the noise of the separate-self diminishes, relational dramas wind down. Greater understanding tends to undermine our personal soap operas and shorten their duration when they arise. Lynn Marie Lumiere offers an illuminating exploration of how spiritual awakening impacts relationships, including a description from Adyashanti of how certain relational issues resolved when he realized his true nature.

> In my experience, what fell away with awakening . . .
> was being attached to my point of view. Which meant
> that I could listen much better and not filter what was
> being said to me through . . . my ego. Making any sort
> of emotional demands on people also fell away. I was
> no longer looking to be fulfilled through or by anyone,
> which paradoxically makes being together much more
> enjoyable. . . . I now experience everyone as an aspect
> of myself. It's a profound sense of spiritual intimacy
> that never wavers.[3]

How would it feel to let go of your point of view? What would it be like to stop making emotional demands on others? What's it like to perceive other people as an aspect of your self?

It's liberating to acknowledge without judgment how we actually function in relationships. Doing so allows us to clearly see through patterns of conditioning that are based on confusion so we can take happiness into our own hands. Imagine the freedom that results from no longer believing that you will be happy and peaceful only when your partner or close friend finally changes his or her annoying behavior or point of view.

Self-righteous blaming tends to be our default position; however, carefully documented research shows that we optimize our relationships by accepting others as they are, rather than trying to change them. People naturally change when they feel accepted. Pioneering marriage researcher John Gottman notes:

People can change only if they feel that they are basically liked and accepted the way they are. When people feel criticized, disliked, and unappreciated they are unable to change. Instead, they feel under siege and dig in to protect themselves.[4]

I addressed this principle earlier in the book. Attuned acceptance fosters natural transformation. Of course, if our partner or friend is truly abusive, we will need to set clear boundaries and leave the relationship if these are not honored. No matter what, relationships are extraordinary learning opportunities for both spiritual insight and emotional maturity, offering us endless opportunities to compassionately observe our egocentricity. Rather than being an obstacle, they are an integral part of our spiritual practice.

Do I Relate from Lack or Fullness?

Most of us unconsciously approach our relationships from a sense of lack—a feeling of not being *enough*—and a hope that others will fill us. We regularly feel that we are not good, lovable, acceptable, pretty, smart, interesting, thin, young, wealthy, . . . not *something* enough. I touched on this theme in chapter 7 in the section on core limiting beliefs. A variation of this belief is that something is *wrong* with the way that I am—for example, *I am fundamentally flawed, damaged, or wounded.*

We often believe that we are both lacking and flawed. These core limiting beliefs are common bedfellows as well as the grandparents of everything that we imagine is missing or wrong about us, and they contribute to an ongoing sense of shame and unworthiness. I invite you here to take a compassionate look at your own beliefs with the following practice. As before, make sure you pause between the steps, and take as long as you need to complete the exercise.

MEDITATIVE INQUIRY
Lack, Flaw, and Unworthiness

Find a time and place where you won't be interrupted, sit comfortably, close your eyes, and take a few deep breaths.

Bring your attention to the heart area and imagine that you can breathe directly into and out of this area.

Ask yourself if you have the belief and feeling that you are fundamentally lacking, flawed, or unworthy. If so, notice the feelings and sensations that go with this belief.

Keeping your attention in your heart area, ask yourself, "What is my deepest knowing about this?" Be quiet. Don't go to your mind for an answer.

Be open to the emergence of a deeper truth and let it in.

~

Yesterday as I was guiding one of my clients through a similar form of this inquiry, he uncovered a twelve-year-old boy within himself who thought and felt that there was a right way to do things that he had never learned. Further, he believed that even if he knew this right way, he probably wouldn't be able to act on it. He had learned these lessons from his father. As a result, he felt ashamed, unworthy, slightly nauseous, and ungrounded.

However, when he invoked his deepest knowing, it came in the form of a wise inner father who told him (his son) that no one really knows what the right way to act is, even if they pretend to. He acknowledged that the boy was sensitive and bright and would navigate his challenging life in an unconventional but creative way. This was the truthful medicine that the boy needed to hear. As the light of awareness elegantly entered into this dark compartment of confusion, my client's feeling of shame and unworthiness quickly dissolved. He felt grounded, clear, and present, knowing that it was enough to take the next obvious step in his life.

We often try to compensate for our unworthiness by asserting an opposite image and story. Instead of being lacking or flawed, we tell our self and others that we are fine, good, or even special in some way. But because we don't truly feel this way, our need for reassurance remains insatiable. As one of my mentees recently described it, the inner gerbil keeps spinning on his wheel, frantically trying to find some path that will prove his specialness once and for all. When the gerbil finally sees the futility of his quest, he comes to a bewildered stop. My client's mind discovered its limit and thereby uncovered an openness to experience that which is neither special nor not special. Can you sense what is prior to affirmation or negation? Who are you before you identify with any story about yourself, positive or negative?

While some public figures with narcissistic personality disorders nakedly act out their desperate image maintenance project through deceit, bullying, and flattery, most of us have our own subtle version of the same. Do you ever edit your narrative to put yourself in a more favorable light or feel wounded when others do not recognize you? If so, explore the underlying motive and belief that drives this tendency. You will bump into some version of lack or flaw.

Most of how we think and feel about our self comes from how we were treated as a child. While we are naturally resilient and respond to relational environments differently based on our temperament, the influence of early parenting is enormous. In the first chapter of my previous book, I outlined the four major attachment (bonding) styles—secure, anxious, avoidant, and disorganized—that researchers have discovered after decades of study. These ways of relating become templates that strongly influence our adult relationships. They can evolve over time, but it takes loving attention and usually some form of a reparative relationship.

When we discover that we are not essentially lacking or
flawed, we stop unconsciously looking to others to fill us.

Do you have the sense that others hold your value and that your well-being depends on their recognition of you? While many of us would say no to that question, we often act otherwise. A good way to tell is to notice whether we look up to others or down at them. If we do, it means that we are projecting our idealized or devalued sense of self onto them. Projection is an unconscious process that shows up most clearly in our waking relationships as well as in our dreams.

As a personal example, during the late 1990s, I had a series of dreams in which I was a valued personal adviser to President Clinton. I would awaken from these dreams with a sense of self-esteem that was conferred by his interest in my counsel. I felt flattered to be sought out by such a powerful person. Not surprisingly, these dreams ended as I came more into conscious contact with my inner authority—I no longer needed to imagine that I was close to a president in order to feel empowered. The projection spontaneously resolved and was replaced by a quiet inner confidence and self-trust.

As we recognize who we really are, we discover that no one is essentially above or below us. We naturally admire and appreciate real talent, expertise, and the qualities of character in others, but that doesn't make them better than us. The opposite is also true. No matter how immature and confused others may appear or how destructively they may act, we know that these same capacities are within us. Everyone is a mirror—the liar, the thief, and the murderer—and these shadowy aspects within us come out under duress and in our dreams. All people deserve kindness and respect, even if they do not act with those qualities toward others.[5]

The conscious recognition of our true nature on the level of the heart brings a sense of inner fullness. When we discover that we are not essentially lacking or flawed, we stop unconsciously looking to others to fill us. Despite our yearning, no one can do this for us, and it was never their job to do so in the first place. Rather, it's our job to discover that our holes come with a hidden *w*. When we approach apparent holes as potential portals and go all the way into and through them, we discover our *w*holeness. And when we directly face and feel the essential core of our apparent lack or flaw, we finally realize that we were never truly a wounded beggar.

As we take responsibility for our own happiness, we stop unconsciously trying to manipulate others. Notice how the following statements strike you. Do they ring true, or do they evoke resistance? Take your time to ponder them. Some may have more charge than others.

> I appreciate that you accept and love me . . .
> and I know that I am acceptable and lovable as I am.
>
> I enjoy being seen and heard by you . . .
> and I am able to see and hear myself.
>
> I love that you are here with me . . .
> and I do not feel abandoned when you go.
>
> I enjoy being by myself . . .
> and I love when you are near.
>
> I love to be held . . .
> and I am able to hold myself and you.
>
> I am not always right . . .
> and I can listen to and learn from you.
>
> I love telling and hearing the truth . . .
> and I am willing to see where it takes us.

These statements are probes. They illuminate how we fundamentally relate with others. I invite you to see how they apply to your close relationships with your partner, friends, and family members.

Byron Katie's *The Work* shines a brilliant light on how we project our desires, hopes, and fears onto others. Her approach invites us to recognize and withdraw our projections—"eliminating the middleman," as she puts it—and to take responsibility for our happiness by getting out of the business of trying to manipulate others.[6] I highly recommend it as a method for recognizing and unwinding your judgments of others.

~ Thirteen ~

THE HEART IN RELATIONSHIP II

Connection, Aloneness, Self-Judgment
and Acceptance, and Listening

For the fierce curve of our lives is moving again to the depths
out of sight, in the deep dark living heart.

D. H. LAWRENCE, *The Complete Poems of D. H. Lawrence*

AS WE ENGAGE the awakening process, one of our most common fears is that we will lose our connection with others. This seems especially true for women. It is true that our relationships simplify and clarify. As we let go of our ordinary identity as a lacking, flawed, or separate self, our way of relating to others changes. We tend to lose interest in more superficial, less authentic ways of being together. We invest less energy in our own self-limiting stories, as well as the self-limiting stories of others. Personal dramas, gossip, and projections tend to fall away, and we spend less time ruminating about the past or anticipating the imagined future. We are more at ease with silence and don't feel compelled to fill the gaps. We realize that we don't need to leave our self in order to meet someone else. In fact, we come to see that until we are at home in our self, we can't truly connect with others.

When there is nothing to prove or disprove about our self, we are more in the present moment, enjoying what is here now. There is creative space for sharing and discovery. Our ordinary life continues, but our relationship to our life becomes increasingly more spacious and open. When someone sincerely asks, "How are you?" it becomes an opportunity for self-inquiry. When we ask another how they are, we actually want to know and we truly listen to their response. Once we taste the clear, sweet waters of *presence*, all other drinks lose their allure.

This shift radiates out into all of our relationships—those that are inauthentic either change or fall away. Some friends and family members may become interested and inspired by the opening they sense unfolding in us, but since our process of self-recognition is not about adopting new beliefs or trying to convince others, we don't feel a need to proselytize. Unfolding presence speaks for itself. If people are sensitive, they will notice; if they are interested, they will inquire. However, many may not, and as our life turns toward what is most essential, this may present some difficult dilemmas.

As our mind and heart open,
our scope of acceptance widens.

How do we navigate a consensual social reality based on the presumption of a separate-self when this no longer is our experience? Do we step back and isolate ourselves? How do we relate with others who show no interest in discovering their true nature? Do we pretend that we are still a separate-self in order get along? These questions can arise most sharply when we revisit our families of origin or childhood friends and are viewed through their familiar lenses. When this occurs, we may feel a strong unconscious pull to reidentify with our old stories and images—a temporary regressive trance. While these experiences can be discouraging, they are also rich opportunities to notice how we unenlighten ourselves.

The process of awakening is fueled by an inner fire that is often not consciously shared by others. Their inner kindling may need to further dry before the spiritual fire ignites, and it's a mystery why some people are ready for this ignition and others are not. Regardless, it's clear that the process cannot be forced. If our partner, friends, or family members aren't called in the same way that we are and if these relationships remain honest and loving, no outer changes are needed. Some people are not consciously interested in the awakening process, but they're supportive and loving just the same. They may even be easier to be with than we are!

As our mind and heart open, our scope of acceptance widens. As noted earlier, we become less attached to our beliefs, make fewer emotional demands, and increasingly see others as aspects of our self. All of our relationships tend to flower, and when some people do prove somewhat challenging to be with, we're better able to view them as our teachers.

Some relationships, however, will be inauthentic or unfitting, and these will require change. It may become clear to us that our long-time partner is a friend rather than a lover. Old friends may fall away. We may need to spend less time with our relatives or not see them at all for a while. We might need to speak and hear difficult truths and end long-standing dysfunctional patterns. This process can be temporarily difficult as we come into clearer alignment with our inner knowing.

In time, these changes will be kinder to everyone. Love and wisdom will disrupt any way of relating that isn't in accord with the truth. We may wind up with fewer friends, but those who remain will be closer than before. Along the way we will find more congruent friends.

But what is real connection? As long as we think of our self as an object—as some *thing*—we will relate to others as objects as well. We will remain merely an image relating to another image—a story that interacts with another story. Is this genuine connection? I think I know who I am and who you are, and you think you know who you are and who I am, yet none of us are who we think we are. How strange! Yet if I know that I am no thing, I am open, and so are you. Most of the time, we just go about our life trying to engage with our mutually imaginary constructs in a consensual virtual reality. Certainly we share thoughts, feelings, sensations, and experiences with others and also play our roles as parent or child, teacher or student, sibling, lover, friend, colleague, acquaintance, or so-called stranger. But are we relating and connecting in the deepest way? I invite you to look into this with the following practice.

Find a time and place where you won't be interrupted, sit comfortably, close your eyes, and take a few deep breaths.

Bring your attention to the heart area and imagine that you can breathe directly into and out of this area.

Ask yourself: "What is real connection? What is my deepest knowing about this?" Be quiet. Don't go to your mind for an answer.

Be open to the emergence of a deeper truth. Let it in.

~

When we truly engage with this inquiry, we discover that we have never *not* been connected. We are unimaginably linked to the whole of life, beyond anything that the separate-self can conceive of. We discover that we are so connected that even the concept of connection falls away. This revelation provides us a foundation and context for all of our relationships.

Knowing that we are all different wave forms of the same ocean gives us a profound sense of space and freedom. We have the felt sense that we are all held by something greater and, furthermore, that we are also that which holds us. Our relationships can breathe, grow, and find their authentic forms. We hold our roles more lightly and, as a result, become more functional and creative within them. We are spontaneously more open, honest, kind, and generous with those around us, but we are also able to set clear boundaries when they are called for. We share our inner radiance more freely because it is intrinsically joyful to do so.

Aloneness

Our greatest suffering comes from our sense of aloneness. Aloneness has two distinct dimensions: psychodynamic and existential—that is, our specific psychological conditioning and the human condition that we all share. If we experienced an early rupture in bonding with our primary caregivers, we're usually left with a strong feeling of interpersonal aloneness on a psychological level. Imagine an infant reaching out to connect with her mother, needing to be touched, warmed, comforted, soothed, nourished, emotionally attuned with, and protected, and instead not finding it—or worse, being shamed or rejected even for reaching out in the first place. Imagine this young child doing so repeatedly, sometimes desperately, and rarely being met or, if so, inconsistently or with confusing conditions.

What's the effect of all of this? It depends on the degree and frequency of the misattunement, neglect, or abuse as well as the child's temperament. Infants will generally first rage and then give up, withdraw, shut down, and try to self-soothe. However, absent the stabilizing presence of an attuned caregiver, their nervous systems remain hyperaroused. They fail to thrive and experience a profound sense of being inconsolably alone. You may have seen and heard this phenomenon in puppies and kittens that are weaned too soon. It's heartbreaking to witness with babies of any kind.

Some of my clients have gone through versions of this type of parenting. It takes years for their systems to unwind and repattern. Even though they feel desperately alone, they also fear opening up to others and risking rejection. To them, it can feel like a matter of life or death to try again. It feels almost impossible to trust another person and cultivate closeness. However, when they are able to do so, it feels profoundly liberating. Being able to authentically connect with another human being feels like coming out of a hellish underground dungeon and into the bright daylight. It takes time, often years, for this contact to happen and for lasting trust to form. It also requires skillful therapists or patient and loving partners who are willing to meet these people in hell without becoming lost there themselves.

When the separate–inside–self—
the little me—is unveiled as timeless awareness,
the bubble of separation bursts.

The other dimension of aloneness I mentioned above is existential. Regardless of our psychological background and attachment style, we feel alone as long as we mis-take our self as a separate-inside-self. Separation = aloneness. There's no way around it, even if we endlessly distract and numb ourselves. This is particularly acute in individualistic societies such as the United States where the fabric of community is increasingly frayed. The angst of the separate-self is magnified as family and community affiliations wither.

This type of aloneness shows up in our terror of death and disability, our fear of being a social outcast, and our need to be seen as a valued member of society. We see it also in our traditional religious beliefs as we attempt to make sense out of apparently random events. It's also evident in our attempts to manipulate others so that we feel safe and loved or, at the very least, not disapproved of. We experience this aloneness as a subtle groundlessness, sensing that everything can be ripped apart at any moment.

MEDITATIVE INQUIRY
Aloneness

Be quiet and take a few deep breaths.

Imagine that you can breathe directly into and out of the heart area.

Ask yourself: "Am I alone? What is my deepest knowing about this?" Don't go to your mind for an answer.

Allow a deeper truth to emerge and let it in.

~

This sense of existential aloneness shifts as we discover the ground of being. When the separate-inside-self—the little me—is unveiled as timeless awareness, the bubble of separation bursts. We recognize that we are not just this story and image, these emotions, and this body. Rather, our thoughts, feelings, and sensations are in us as open awareness, and they are intimate expressions of who we really are. When we realize that we are a wave *and* the ocean, the existential dimension of aloneness dissolves.

Judging Our Self and Others

Judgments poison relationships and promote disconnection precisely 100 percent of the time. Check it out for yourself. Think of someone that you critically judge, consciously evoke your judgment of them, and then notice if you feel closer to or more distant from that person.

Discernment means seeing things as they are. Judgment means evaluating whether something or someone is good or bad, right or wrong. We can detect our judgments by the use of *should* in our thought and speech. When we judge, we're measuring what is actual against an ideal—for example, we tell our self that someone *should not* have done something when in fact they did. Our conditioned mind is arguing with reality, which is something that it does particularly well.

When we tap into presence,
we realize that we are already accepted as we are.

All judgments of others start with self-judgments. The less conscious we are, the more we project these self-judgments onto others. For example, if I think that someone else is truly bad, nasty, or evil, I hold some version of the same judgment about myself, usually subconsciously. Because we can't bear this feeling about our self, we project it onto others. Taking responsibility for these projections doesn't mean that we become blind to the harm that others do or that we are paralyzed from taking appropriate action. It does mean that we stop moralizing and pretending that we are essentially separate from anyone else.

As we recognize and see through the shadow elements in our own psyche, we stop projecting them onto others. We all have weaknesses and blind spots, and the more we can accept our self as we are without judgment, the more we will accept others just as they are. With genuine self-acceptance, it becomes impossible to sustain negative judgments of others. We naturally do unto others as we do unto our self. We stop casting stones both inwardly and outwardly.

Radical Acceptance of Self and Other

How do we accept our self? Here is a hint: we don't. At least, our ordinary mind doesn't, despite our best intentions. Our conditioned mind is designed to judge and compare, so to expect it to accept unconditionally is both unrealistic and unkind. Presented with the injunction to accept what is, the mind will judge itself for being too judgmental—talk about a paradox. My mother would call this a real kettle of fish.

The paradox resolves when we recognize that radical acceptance of our self and others comes from somewhere other than the conditioned mind. It comes from presence—the conscious recognition of being. When we tap into presence, we realize that we are already accepted as we are. We don't have to work at it, we just need to recognize it.

At the end of a recent retreat, I guided a meditation in which I invited everyone to recognize that they were completely loved and accepted as they were—there was nothing to fix, change, or attain that would make them any more whole than they already were. During our closing circle, one of the participants, who had been notably quiet the prior four days, said that this particular meditation had touched her the most. She realized that she had long been holding the belief that if anyone really got to know her, they would find out that she was neither lovable nor acceptable and then abandon her. Letting this core belief go was a huge relief for her.

Radical Acceptance

Take a few deep breaths and relax.

Breathe directly into and out of the heart area.

Ask yourself: "Is there something that already accepts me as I am?" Sense what comes as you keep an open mind.

Open to being completely accepted just as you are.

~

Spiritual Awakening and Emotional Maturity

I once believed that spiritual awakening would guarantee emotional maturity. Unfortunately, it doesn't—at least not at first. For some, this maturity never happens. We can be aware that we are aware and yet be emotionally in the dark. Even as we may become conscious of the *context* of our experience, we can remain unaware of our subconscious and emotional *content*.

> *When we are willing to shed our conditioned armoring,*
> *we uncover the luminous resilience in the core of our being.*

This disparity is common in contemplative traditions that largely emphasize observing experience—just noticing passing thoughts and sensations in some Buddhist practices for example or actively disidentifying from those thoughts and sensations in classic Advaita Vedanta. This kind of guidance encourages a sense of detachment, clarity, inner spaciousness, and freedom, but it can also enable emotional coldness and relational distancing when people use these practices—consciously or otherwise—to avoid their feelings.

Transcendentally oriented practitioners tend to identify with being a witness, a no one, or as spacious, pure awareness itself. Men tend to do this more than women, but both genders easily fall into the trap. Once we have consciously recognized the big space of open awareness, it's easy to hide out there—if we have touched something infinitely spacious, why muck around with messy emotions and relationships? The rationale to avoid feelings can be strong, and there's little incentive to be emotionally vulnerable.

Our subtle belief systems govern how we relate to our experience. So does our honesty and willingness to be vulnerable. If we have an immanent approach to life, we know that the finite is not separate from the infinite, and we recognize that stepping back from experience, while important, is incomplete. We know that we also need to at times step into and through our experience, which means that we need to intimately embrace our subjective experience as it is, including all of our inner feelings and sensations as they arise. Anything less is dualistic and incomplete.

At times this more intimate approach can be uncomfortable and destabilizing. It's important to ask ourselves what's more important to us: comfort or the truth? Emotional vulnerability is a form of self-honesty. It's also a portal to a genuine core strength. When we are willing to shed our conditioned armoring, we uncover the luminous resilience in the core of our being.

Emotional maturity means that we take responsibility for our emotions. If we find ourselves emotionally shut down or triggered, we don't dismiss or ignore our state, nor do we launch into another self-improvement project to fix ourselves, knowing that we are already whole.

Our honesty and willingness to be vulnerable allows us to explore our conditioning as it arises, particularly reactive patterns. We are willing to sense our body, feel our feelings, and be curious about any underlying subconscious beliefs that might be fueling our reactions. This openness allows the emotional and instinctual domains—the heart and the hara—to come more into conscious awareness and align with our inner knowing. It supports the process of *waking down*. As we open to fear, grief, anger, and shame, they begin to unfold, transform, and integrate. Essential energies are liberated and come into service to a greater whole.

Emotional maturity allows us to enter into truly adult relationships with others. As our feelings become more fluid, balanced, and accessible, we can use them to intimately and empathically connect with others. We are better able to share our love, joy, grief, appreciation, and gratitude without inhibition. As we embrace our feelings, we also come into more conscious relationship with the younger parts of our self, our inner children who were frozen and stuffed away early on. This in turn frees essential qualities of our humanity: courage, power, vitality, and innocence. Emotional maturity also allows greater understanding and compassion for others as well as more intimacy.

Some people possess significant emotional maturity, but they've yet to recognize their true nature as infinite awareness. Others have attained spiritual clarity but lack emotional maturity. Having both is clearly preferable.

Soulful Relating

When we are consciously aware of awareness, we are available to relate as presence with everyone (and everything) that we meet. In essence, we meet our self everywhere, all of the time. This is the great intimacy—the nonlocalized Heart meeting itself.

Your closest kindred spirit is yourself.

There is another kind of meeting that can take place on the level of the soul—a subtle level that we can sometimes sense at the back of the heart area (as I described in chapter 2). This archetypal level is linked to the expression of essential qualities of being—joy, innocence, courage, gratitude, love, and insight—with a unique individual flavor, a specific vibratory quality. It's the sweetest and most profound level of individual meeting.

When two people meet on this wavelength, they both enjoy a sense of intense resonance. It feels like we have known this person our whole life and perhaps in past ones, if they exist. It may take time for this soul-level relating to come into conscious awareness, or it can happen immediately. This resonance can happen between friends and lovers and between teachers and their students. It has an abiding quality that does not feel dependent upon space or time—we can feel this intimate bond regardless of physical proximity. It may include intellectual, emotional, or erotic intimacy, but this level of resonance does not depend on any particular channel of expression.

I suspect that the myth of the *soul mate* arises from meetings of this type. Personally, I don't believe that we have only one soul mate. This degree of intimacy is about the quality of the meeting, rather than a specific individual. There is a pool of kindred spirits—masculine, feminine, nonbinary, and otherwise—with whom we can profoundly resonate. The more in touch we are with this level within our self, the more available we are to meet others in this way. If you want to find your soul mates and recognize them as you cross paths, you can start by looking in the mirror. Your closest kindred spirit is yourself.

The Gift of Listening

For many years I taught a course entitled "The Art of Listening" to master's level counseling students, who regularly told me that it was one of the most important classes of their graduate training and that the positive effects of the course radiated out beyond their clinical work into their personal relationships as well. During the class, students focused on learning to simply *be* with others from deep silence and an open heart—in other words, from presence, without an agenda to fix or change anyone. They also discovered how to listen with their whole body, including an energetic level that resonated with their clients' interior experience. They learned that this capacity to attune with others facilitates empathy and a natural unfolding of discovery and healing.

Deep listening is rare. We light up when we are on the receiving end of it, and are often surprised when someone pays careful attention to us. In truth, most of us don't listen well because we are lost in our own story. I invite you to take a day to focus on carefully listening to others and notice what gets in the way of truly hearing them. Notice, too, how they respond when you listen in this way.

Often we can't wait for the other person to stop speaking so we can assert our point of view and draw attention back to our self. We quickly compare what we are hearing to experiences we've had in the past and then want to describe those experiences to others. We also tend to judge others and dismiss their experience, inadvertently or otherwise, or are quick to give advice in the name of being helpful. In sum, we get caught up in our own thinking and wrapped up in our own story. This type of listening comes from the conditioned mind. It's rarely creative, interesting, or all that helpful.

To listen to another from presence means to listen from spacious, open, loving awareness. When we do so, we don't listen through our agendas of trying to change them—we already know that they are fundamentally whole and not essentially separate from ourselves. We also know that they have the answers to their own pressing questions. Furthermore, they *are* the answer.

There are multiple levels of listening: mental, emotional, energetic, and essential. When we listen carefully to another person on a mental level, we are able to grasp their central narrative, make cognitive sense of what they are saying, and accurately reflect it back to them. This kind of clarity and insight fosters their self-understanding. Even if we don't share their perspective, we're able to step into it.

When we listen to others on an emotional level, we're able to feel their feelings to some degree and accurately empathize with them. This fosters a sense of greater intimacy and understanding, enriching the feeling of connection. Similarly, listening on an energetic level means that we step into a subtle, interior realm of contact with others, which they may or may not be in touch with in themselves, and this level of resonance further enhances and illumines their sense of self-intimacy and self-understanding.

Finally, when we listen from the level of being or *essence*, we feel that we are listening to our self. We receive the gift of the other's being with genuine appreciation. And when we are able to meet others with several dimensions of listening, an initial exchange of ideas may transform into an unexpected and profoundly touching experience of simply being together.

Deep listening is innocent and happens moment to moment. It's comfortable not knowing what comes next and does not have a goal or conclusion. It loves both silence and creative discovery and does not have a story to tell or an image to assert. Listening of this kind is open-minded, warm-hearted, open-bodied, grounded, peaceful, sometimes humorous, empathic, and curious. It invites clarity, intimacy, and love into the foreground of awareness. It is the greatest gift that we can offer to each other.

~ Fourteen ~

CONCLUSION

Coming Home to the Deep Heart

The spiritual task we are given is a simple one:
to attend to that inner spark of radiance,
to hold vigil over it until we realize it to be our self,
and to dig up and cast off all argument we have with its love.
ADYASHANTI

IN THE INTRODUCTION, I suggested that we are all knowingly or unknowingly on a spiritual pilgrimage from the head to the heart. One way or another, we are trying to find our way home. Some of us come on our knees humbled after struggling to find happiness in the world, whereas others are directly called by the light of our true nature. Whether pushed or pulled, something in the core of our being reaches out and draws us in. We turn toward the glow of our true nature and begin to tend the inner fire.

There are three broad stages in this pilgrimage. First, we attend to this radiance with increasing intimacy and devotion. Second, we recognize that this radiant presence is who we fundamentally are, rather than merely a beneficent state of being—our mind, heart, and gut awaken to the infinite. Finally, we align our daily lives with our deepest knowing. This last step is ongoing and open-ended. These stages can also be viewed as *orienting toward, awakening to,* and increasingly *embodying* our true nature.

We need to be able to recognize, question,
and see through the illusions of all
of our constraining self-images and stories.

The first phase of the conscious spiritual journey is to orient to a deeper reality. We start to intuit something silent and sacred in the midst of our busy and challenging lives—perhaps we've come across profound books or inspirational teachers or we simply resonate in an uncommon way when we hear a friend express themselves genuinely and openly. Maybe we begin to meditate or experiment with silent prayer. We start to sit with existential questions such as, Who am I, really? What is it that I most value in life? and What is most important? We begin to pay more careful attention to our actual experience and question all of our commonsense assumptions about who we are and what the world is. We find ourselves drawn to spend quiet time in nature and to have more authentic conversations with others. We ponder the foundational teachings of our religious faith, if we have one, or take time off from work and family responsibilities to go on a spiritual retreat. As we tend the inner flame in this way, we become more attuned to its light and warmth.

This radiance looks and feels a little different for each of us. Some other images that express our essential nature include prisms, embers, diamonds, clear springs, or hives of golden bees (from Antonio Machado's poem "Last Night as I Was Sleeping"). These images, direct from the psyche, correspond with essential qualities of being: wisdom, clarity, love, kindness, compassion, gratitude, generosity, courage, inner strength and stability, joy, awe, wonder, delight, contentment, and peace. To use yet another image, they're like rays emitting from an inner sun that we can follow back to their source.

To turn toward something requires that we turn away from something else. Above all, this means turning away from our conditioned identity—who we think and feel that we are. We need to be able to recognize, question, and see through the illusions of all of our constraining self-images and stories. To be filled, we must first be emptied. To come home, we must leave the apparent comfort and safety of our self-construct. This requires honesty, courage, and keen discernment. Above all, it requires the love of truth prior to thought.

It is critically important to differentiate awareness from thought. Whatever thoughts we are having are happening *in* awareness. Without awareness, there is no thought. Without thought, there is still awareness. As we recognize this experiential truth and gain space from our thoughts, especially judgmental ones, attention is freed to make the great pilgrimage from the head to the heart and beyond.

As we are able to see through our stories and discern awareness from thought, our attention steadies and our sense of self clarifies. We are less easily distracted and confused, and a virtuous cycle emerges. The more attention we give to the essential, the more it comes into the foreground of awareness, and the dialogue between our conditioned mind and our unconditioned nature becomes increasingly intimate. The moth draws to the flame of inner knowing in ever closer circles.

Resistance inevitably arises. We fear the unknown and unknowingly project our worst fears onto it: annihilation, aloneness, deadness, disconnection, engulfment, madness, or disability. We gradually face and step through our fears and confusion, and—at some point, always unexpectedly—we experience a shift, perhaps as subtle as the Amazon River as it blends into the Atlantic Ocean or as obvious as Yosemite Falls cascading over the cliff. In either case, a profound and enduring recognition of the infinite nature of awareness occurs. I use the passive voice to describe this shift because it does not belong or refer to anyone. No one wakes up; awareness awakens to itself. This shift or opening is accompanied by a sense of spaciousness and inner freedom. Often this recognition happens first on the level of the mind as a mental awakening.

We were never fundamentally lacking,
flawed, or separate.
We find an inherent wholeness
that was always in plain sight.

We might continue to seek on a subtle feeling level. It's the tendency of the mind to make our true nature into an object and then search for it like a miner who fears they've missed the gold rush. We mistakenly think that what we seek is an inner state, so our prospecting will inevitably fail because what we seek is not an object like a glimmering nugget of gold in a stream. Instead, what we're looking for is the one who is looking.

When the encircling moth finally meets the flame, it does not burn to death. Rather, it discovers that it was always a flame in disguise. It becomes an illumined moth-flame. The apparent separate-self is unveiled *as* the light of awareness—a radical, transformative insight. The joke is on us. It is hard to describe the humor and relief that comes from the discovery that we are the one we have been looking for and that we are no one and everything.

Our true nature is *not* a special state that comes and goes—we simply recognize what has always been here, silently embedded within every experience. Our ancient pilgrimage ends in the timeless now, in presence. We were never fundamentally lacking, flawed, or separate. We find an inherent wholeness that was always in plain sight, and the discovery brings inner freedom, peace, quiet joy, and a sense of intimacy with the whole of life.

A subtle duality may persist between a sense of self that feels whole and an outer world that seems separate—that is, between an infinite *knower* and a finite *known*. In time, we recognize that our true nature as loving awareness is the source and substance of everyone and everything, and this discovery dissolves the final duality. There is only *knowing*. This is the awakening of the Deepest Heart, the revelation of essential love, and the flowering of presence.

The process of discovery and unfolding continues even as the search for the essential ends. Reactions stored in our body-mind will inevitably arise. As Adya so eloquently puts it, our final task is to "dig up and cast off" our remaining argument with the love that is inherent within this radiance.

When we are honest with ourselves, our arguments tend to unearth themselves, most often in the arena of relationships but also in the form of unresolved traumas. When they do get flushed out, we are curious and affectionate with them. We don't take them as evidence that our fundamental understanding is mistaken or dismiss them as being unworthy of attention. When confusion is exposed to the light of awareness, it melts like ice—sometimes quickly, at other times slowly. The casting off or melting happens through clear seeing, feeling, and sensing. As a result, the gap between our deepest knowing and our daily life decreases.

Living as Presence

The radiance of the Deep Heart is calling each of us. I invite you to listen and respond. It is your birthright to live in and as presence—the conscious recognition of your being. You are worthy of it by the fact that you exist. There are no exceptions.

At the very end of the Camino de Santiago in Spain, ninety kilometers beyond the Cathedral of St. James, lies Cape Finisterre on the Costa da Morte (Coast of Death). Medieval pilgrims believed that it was the end of the world. Until recently, Camino pilgrims, after walking for hundreds of miles, would burn their clothes and boots on a steep hillside overlooking the ocean as a purification ritual. At sunset, they would stand before the vast sea—barefoot, stripped, and open.

Your life is a spiritual pilgrimage into the Deep Heart. I invite you to approach the ocean of the unknown and to see through the rags of your conditioned identity. They disguise your native innocence and wholeness.

I wish you well on your journey into the Heart of Presence.

NOTES

INTRODUCTION

1. While the phenomenon called spiritual bypassing is real, the term is a misnomer. If *spirit* refers to our true nature as loving awareness, then spirit is all-inclusive and cannot bypass anything.

CHAPTER 1

1. I am grateful to Rupert Spira for this useful and precise formulation found in *Presence: The Art of Peace and Happiness—Volume 1* (Salisbury, UK: Nonduality Press, 2011).
2. Alan Watts, *The Book on the Taboo of Knowing Who You Are* (New York: Vintage Books, Reissue Edition, 1989).

CHAPTER 2

1. Robert W. Mitchell, "Evidence of Dolphin Self-Recognition and the Difficulties of Interpretation," *Consciousness and Cognition* 4, no. 2: 229–34; Rebecca Turner, "10 Animals with Self Awareness," World of Lucid Dreaming, world-of-lucid-dreaming.com/10-animals-with -self-awareness.html.
2. Nisargadatta Maharaj, *I Am That*, 2nd American ed. (Durham, NC: Acorn Press, 2012), 204.
3. Victor Sogen Hori, "The Steps of Koan Practice," in *Sitting with Koans: Essential Writings on Zen Koan Instrospection*, ed. John Daido Loori and Thomas Yuho Kirchner (Somerville, MA: Wisdom Publications, 2006).
4. Eckart Tolle, *The Power of Now* (Novato, CA: New World Library, 2004); Christin Weber, *A Cry in the Desert: The Awakening of Byron Katie* (London: The Work Foundation, 1996); Joel Morwood, *Naked Through the Gate*, 2nd ed. (Eugene, OR: The Center for Sacred Sciences, 2012); Suzanne Segal, *Collision with the Infinite* (San Diego: Blue Dove Press, 1996).

CHAPTER 3

1. David Godman, *Be as You Are: The Teachings of Ramana Maharshi* (London: Arkana, 1985).
2. Jean Klein, public talk, Berkeley, CA, 1989.
3. Adyashanti, "True Meditation," 2011, adyashanti.org/teachings /intro-teachings#ot_true-meditation, accessed January 25, 2019.

CHAPTER 4

1. Eugene Gendlin, *Focusing*, 2nd ed. (New York: Bantam Books, 1982).
2. Potential questions are: (1) Who or what are you, really? (2) What is the most important thing? (3) Where are you, right now? (4) When are you? (5) What is the true nature of the heart? (followed by) Does it need to be protected? (6) What is your deepest ground? (7) How does your deepest truth want to move in your life? (8) What is your deepest knowing? (9) What is this?

CHAPTER 5

1. Jonathan N. Tinsley, Maxim I. Molodtsov, Robert Prevedel, David Wartmann, Jofre Espigulé-Pons, Mattais Lauwers, and Alipasha Vaziri, "Direct Detection of a Single Photon by Humans," Nature Communications 7 (July 19, 2016), nature.com/articles /ncomms12172.
2. Jaideva Singh, *Vijnanabhairava or Divine Consciousness: A Treasury of 112 Types of Yoga* (New Delhi: Motilal Banarsidass, 2002).
3. Stephan Bodian, "An Interview with Jean Klein," *Yoga Journal* 83 (November/December 1988), o-meditation.com/2009/11/28 /an-interview-with-jean-klein-2/.
4. Jean Klein, notes from a private talk. Santa Barbara, CA, 1992.

CHAPTER 6

1. For a linguistic and historic definition of tantra, please see Georg Feuerstein's *Tantra: The Path of Ecstacy* (Boston: Shambhala, 1998). For a comprehensive overview of Kashmiri Nondual Shaivism, see Christopher Wallis's *Tantra Illuminated: The Philosophy, History, and Practice of a Timeless Tradition* (Petaluma, CA: Mattamayura Press, 2013).

2. Adyashanti, *The End of Your World: Uncensored Straight Talk about the Nature of Enlightenment* (Boulder, CO: Sounds True, 2010).

3. Adyashanti, "Love Returning for Itself," in *The Sacred Mirror*, ed. John Prendergast, Peter Fenner, and Shelia Krystal (St. Paul, MN: Paragon House, 2003).

4. Peter Levine, *Waking the Tiger: Healing Trauma* (Berkeley, CA: North Atlantic, 1997).

5. Richard Miller, *Yoga Nidra: A Meditative Practice for Deep Relaxation and Healing* (Boulder, CO: Sounds True, 2010).

6. Laurel Parnell, *Tapping In: A Step-by-Step Guide for Activating Your Healing Resources Through Bilateral Stimulation* (Boulder, CO: Sounds True, 2008).

CHAPTER 7

1. Hara Estroff Marano, "Our Brain's Negative Bias," *Psychology Today* (June 20, 2003), psychologytoday.com/us/articles/200306/our-brains-negative-bias.

2. Adyashanti, *The Five Truths about Truth* (Campbell, CA: Open Gate Sangha, 2007), audio CD.

3. Byron Katie, *Loving What Is: Four Questions That Can Change Your Life* (New York: Crown Archetype, 2002); Hale Dwoskin, *The Sedona Method: Your Key to Lasting Happiness, Success, Peace, and Emotional Well-Being* (Sedona, AZ: Sedona Press, 2003).

4. Joseph Campbell, *A Hero with a Thousand Faces*, 3rd ed. (Novato, CA: New World Library, 2008).

CHAPTER 8

1. Seung Sahn, *Only Don't Know: Selected Teaching Letters of Zen Master Seung Sahn*, revised, subsequent edition (Boston, MA: Shambhala, 1999).

2. David Godman, *The Teachings of Sri Ramana Maharshi* (London: Arkana, 1985), 77.

CHAPTER 9

1. Bessel Van der Kolk, *The Body Keeps the Score: Brain, Mind, and Body in the Healing of Trauma* (New York: Penguin Books, 2014).

2. Van der Kolk, *The Body Keeps the Score*.

3. A. H. Almaas, *Diamond Heart*, Books 1 and 2 (Boston: Shambhala, 2000).

4. Marshall Silverstein, *Self Psychology and Diagnostic Assessment: Identifying Selfobject Functions Through Psychological Testing* (New York: Routledge, 2014).

5. Chip Brown, "Enlightenment Therapy," *New York Times Magazine* (April 23, 2009), nytimes.com/2009/04/26/magazine/26zen-t.html.

CHAPTER 11

1. For more on this topic, I recommend Judith Blackstone's *Trauma and the Unbound Body: The Healing Power of Fundamental Consciousness* (Boulder, CO: Sounds True, 2018).

2. Jean Klein, *Who Am I? The Sacred Quest* (Dorset, England: Element Books, 1988), 7.

3. Jean Klein, *Transmission of the Flame*, 1st ed., 2nd printing ed. (St. Peter Port, Guernsey: Third Millennium Books, 1994).

4. Robert Sapolsky, *Behave: The Biology of Humans at Our Best and Worst* (New York: Penguin Books, 2018).

5. Yuval Noah Harari, *Sapiens: A Brief History of Humankind* (New York: Harper, 2015).

6. James W. Moore, "What Is the Sense of Agency and Why Does It Matter?" *Frontiers in Psychology* 7 (2016), doi.org/10.3389/fpsyg.2016.01272.

7. Chun Siong Soon, Marcel Brass, Hans-Jochen Heinze, and John-Dylan Haynes, "Unconscious Determinants of Free Decisions in the Human Brain," *Nature Neuroscience* 11, no. 5 (2008): 543–45.

8. Roberto Assagioli, *The Act of Will* (Amherst, MA: The Synthesis Center, 2010).

9. James Bugental, *Psychotherapy and Process: The Fundamentals of an Existential-Humanistic Approach* (New York: McGraw-Hill College, 1978).

CHAPTER 12

1. Jean Klein, *Who Am I?, The Sacred Quest* (Dorset, England: Element Books, 1988) 2.

2. Brian Victoria, *Zen at War* (Oxford: Rowman and Littlefield, 2006).

3. Lynn Marie Lumiere, *Awakened Relating: A Guide to Embodying Undivided Love in Intimate Relationships* (Oakland, CA: Non-Duality Press, 2018), 162.

4. John Gottman, *The Seven Principles for Making Marriages Work: A Practical Guide from the Country's Foremost Relationships Expert* (New York: Harmony, 2015), 157.
5. As a relevant aside, Norway has invested heavily in the humane rehabilitation of its criminals and has experienced a subsequent low rate of recidivism, as compared to that of the United States.
6. Byron Katie, *Loving What Is: Four Questions That Can Change Your Life* (New York: Crown Archetype, 2002).

ADDITIONAL RESOURCES

Adyashanti. *Emptiness Dancing*. Boulder, CO: Sounds True, 2006.

Adyashanti. *Falling into Grace: Insights on the End of Suffering*. Boulder, CO: Sounds True, 2013.

Adyashanti. *The Way of Liberation*. San Jose, CA: Open Gate Sangha, 2013.

Almaas, A. H. *Facets of Unity*. Boston: Shambhala, 2002.

Almaas, A. H. *Runaway Realization*. Boston: Shambhala, 2014.

Almaas, A. H. *The Alchemy of Freedom: The Philosophers' Stone and the Secrets of Existence*. Boulder, CO: Shambhala, 2017.

Almaas, A. H., and Karen Johnson. *The Power of Divine Eros: The Illuminating Force of Love in Everyday Life*. Boston: Shambhala, 2013.

Bodian, Stephan. *Beyond Mindfulness: The Direct Approach to Lasting Peace, Happiness, and Love*. Oakland, CA: Non-Duality Press, 2017.

Bourgeault, Cynthia. *The Wisdom Jesus: Transforming Heart and Mind—A New Perspective on Christ and His Message*. Boulder, CO: Shambhala, 2008.

Bourgeault, Cynthia. *The Heart of Centering Prayer: Nondual Christianity in Theory and Practice*. Boulder, CO: Shambhala, 2016.

Brach, Tara. *Radical Acceptance: Embracing Your Life with a Heart of the Buddha*. New York: Bantam, 2004.

Hanson, Rick. *Hardwiring Happiness: The New Brain Science of Contentment, Calm, and Confidence*. New York: Harmony, 2013.

Johnson, Will. *Rumi: Gazing at the Beloved*. Rochester, VT: Inner Traditions International, 2003.

Kelly, Loch. *Shift into Freedom: The Science and Practice of Open-Hearted Awareness*. Boulder, CO: Sounds True, 2015.

Klein, Jean. *Be Who You Are*. Salisbury, UK: Non-Duality Press, 2006.

Maharshi, Ramana. *Talks with Ramana Maharshi*. San Diego, CA: Inner Directions, 2000.

Miller, Richard. *The iRest Program for Healing PTSD*. Oakland, CA: New Harbinger Publications, 2015.

Morwood, Joel. *The Way of Selflessness: A Practical Guide to Enlightenment Based Upon the World's Great Mystics*. Eugene, OR: Center for Sacred Sciences, 2009.

Prendergast, John, Peter Fenner, and Sheila Krystal, eds. *The Sacred Mirror: Nondual Wisdom and Psychotherapy*. St. Paul, MN: Paragon House, 2003.

Prendergast, John, and Ken Bradford, eds. *Listening from the Heart of Silence: Nondual Wisdom and Psychotherapy*, vol. 2. St. Paul, MN: Paragon House, 2007.

Ray, Reggie. *Touching Enlightenment: Finding Realization in the Body*. Boulder, CO: Sounds True, 2014.

Ray, Reggie. *The Awakening Body: Somatic Meditation for Discovering Our Deepest Life*. Boulder, CO: Shambhala, 2016.

Spira, Rupert. *Transparent Body, Luminous World: The Tantric Yoga of Sensation and Perception* (MP3 CD Set). Oxford: Sahaja Publications, 2015.

Spira, Rupert. *Being Aware of Being Aware*. The Essence of Meditation Series. Oxford: Sahaja Publications, 2017.

Wallis, Christopher. *The Recognition Sutras: Illuminating a 1,000-Year-Old Masterpiece*. Petaluma, CA: Mattamayura Press, 2017.

ACKNOWLEDGMENTS

IT IS A MYSTERY how I wrote this book. It felt as if the whole universe somehow participated in the process. How does one express gratitude to the whole of life? With a sincere bow in all directions and in no direction, and with a heart full of gratitude.

Some specific bows are also in order. First, to my dear wife, Christiane, who hugs and nourishes me, sings to me, and makes me laugh when I am not sequestered for long periods of writing. I am a lucky man!

I also bow to my friends Stephan Bodian, Kelly Boys, Marjorie Bair, and Steve Hadland for their enthusiastic support and helpful feedback.

I offer a deep bow, as well, to Adyashanti, who graciously agreed to write the foreword for this book. My gratitude for his friendship is fathomless.

I bow to Jean Klein as well as to Nisargadatta Maharaj and Ramana Maharshi—each of them master unveilers of the light of awareness.

I bow to Dorothy Hunt, whose friendship, love, support, and decades-long gazing practice together has helped to unlock many sacred chambers of the Deep Heart.

I bow with gratitude to my students and clients, whose courage, vulnerability, and love for the truth endlessly inspire me.

I bow, too, to Tami Simon who, after I completed *In Touch*, intuited that I had a few more books awaiting birth and graciously supported this offering.

I also bow to my Sounds True editor, Robert Lee, for his Manjushri-like clarity as he pruned this manuscript into its final form. Thanks for your masterful editing, Robert!

And a final bow to you, the reader, for whom I wrote this book. The writer and the reader, though different, are not separate. Life is awakening to itself through each of us. Thank you for reading, resonating, and inquiring on your own, and for not going to your mind for an answer!

ABOUT THE AUTHOR

JOHN J. PRENDERGAST, PHD, is the author of *In Touch: How to Tune In to the Inner Guidance of Your Body and Trust Yourself.* He is a retired adjunct professor of psychology at the California Institute of Integral Studies, where he taught and supervised master's level counseling students for twenty-three years. He has been a licensed psychotherapist in private practice since the mid-1980s.

John is the senior editor of and contributor to two anthologies of original essays, *The Sacred Mirror: Nondual Wisdom and Psychotherapy* (with Peter Fenner and Sheila Krystal) and *Listening from the Heart of Silence* (with Ken Bradford).

He studied for many years with the European Advaita master Dr. Jean Klein and also with Adyashanti. John was invited to share the dharma by Dorothy Hunt. He lives in Petaluma, California, and offers retreats in the United States and Europe as well as online talks. For more, please visit listeningfromsilence.com.

ABOUT SOUNDS TRUE

SOUNDS TRUE is a multimedia publisher whose mission is to inspire and support personal transformation and spiritual awakening. Founded in 1985 and located in Boulder, Colorado, we work with many of the leading spiritual teachers, thinkers, healers, and visionary artists of our time. We strive with every title to preserve the essential "living wisdom" of the author or artist. It is our goal to create products that not only provide information to a reader or listener, but that also embody the quality of a wisdom transmission.

For those seeking genuine transformation, Sounds True is your trusted partner. At SoundsTrue.com you will find a wealth of free resources to support your journey, including exclusive weekly audio interviews, free downloads, interactive learning tools, and other special savings on all our titles.

To learn more, please visit SoundsTrue.com/freegifts or call us toll-free at 800.333.9185.

In loving memory of Beth Skelley, book designer extraordinaire.
Her spirit lives on in our books and in our hearts.